Consuming Subjects

Consuming Subjects

Women, Shopping, and Business
in the
Eighteenth Century

Elizabeth Kowaleski-Wallace

COLUMBIA UNIVERSITY PRESS   NEW YORK

Columbia University Press

Publishers Since 1893

New York   Chichester, West Sussex

"China" is reprinted from *Eighteenth-Century Studies*
(1995/1996), 29(2):153–67, by permission of the
publisher, Johns Hopkins University Press, for the
American Society for Eighteenth-Century Studies.

Library of Congress Cataloging-in-Publication Data

Kowaleski-Wallace, Elizabeth.

Consuming subjects : women, shopping, and business

in the eighteenth century / Elizabeth Kowaleski-Wallace.

p. cm.

ISBN 0-231-10578-9. ISBN 0-231-10579-7 (pbk.)

1. Women consumers—Great Britain—18th century.

2. Women consumers—Great Britain—History—19th century.

3. Consumer behavior—Great Britain—History—18th century.

4. Consumer bvehavior—Great Britain—History—19th century.

I. Title.

HC260.C6K69   1996

381'.1'082—dc20   96-22778

CIP

Casebound editions of Columbia University Press
books are printed on permanent and durable
acid-free paper.

Printed in the United States of America

c 10 9 8 7 6 5 4 3 2 1

For my splendid family—Jim, Rebecca, Clarissa, and Ian

Contents

Acknowledgments

This book was written under the auspices of a fellowship from the National Endowment for the Humanities and with assistance from Boston College in the form of a Research Incentive Grant. Many colleagues generously read and commented on portions of the manuscript. I thank Pamela Bromberg, Shelia Conboy, Mary Crane, Deidre Lynch, Helena Michie, Ruth Perry, Sara Quay, Alan Richardson, Sarah Stanbury, and Robyn Warhol. Laura Brown provided incisive commentary and offered very useful suggestions for revision. My children, Clarissa and Ian, taught me to think about consumer culture in still other ways, and I thank them for enthusiastically sharing their knowledge about American Girls dolls. I would have to trace many of the ideas in this book to conversations with Jim Wallace. He has been most generous with time he could barely spare, and, for all his help with this book, I owe him lots of time to listen to opera in peace: "Mi piaccion quelle cose che hansi dolce malia, che parlano d'amor."

Consuming Subjects

Introduction

In *The Expedition of Humphry Clinker* (1771), Lismahago, former soldier of British colonial wars, relays the horrifying tale of his previous captivity among the Miamis.[1] Unlike his companion Murphy, who was "so mangled" by the Miami women and children that "he was rendered altogether unfit for the purposes of marriage," Lismahago—his manhood still intact—is given as a trophy to the "squaw" Squinkinacoosta. While Murphy is literally eaten by his captives, Lismahago is almost metaphorically consumed by his bride. Her appetite is so voracious that "she vied with the stoutest warrior in eating the flesh of the sacrifice." Later, she meets her demise by "eating too much raw bear" (193–194). In a passage that is (presumably) offered as darkly humorous,[2] misogyny and racism intersect. If the squaw represents woman in her most uncivilized form, then her disgusting appetite belongs to woman in her "natural" state.

Within the novel Squinkinacoosta functions as dark other to Tabitha, spinster sister to Matthew Bramble. While Squinkinacoosta makes only a cameo appearance, Tabitha carries the weight throughout the novel for Smollett's own deep antipathy to consumer culture.[3] Tabitha's appetite is linked to Squinkinacoosta's first through her fascination with the Miami woman's costume and later through her perverted taste. While Lismahago is narrating his travails, Tabitha ignores the atrocities committed on the male bodies. Her attention is directed instead to the details of Squinkinacoosta's dress. She demands to know whether Lismahago's bride "wore high-breasted stays or boddice, a robe of silk or velvet, and laces of Mechlin or minionette—she supposed as they were connected with the French, she used *rouge*, and had her hair dressed in the Parisian fashion." But here is what Squinkinacoosta wore:

> Her bridal dress consisted of a petticoat of red bays, and fringed blanket, fastened about her shoulders with a copper skewer; but of ornaments she had plenty.—Her hair was curiously plaited, and interwoven with bobbins of human bone—one eye-lid was painted green, and the other yellow; the cheeks were blue, the lips white, the teeth red, and there was a black list drawn down the middle of her forehead as far as the tip of the nose—a couple of gaudy parrot's feathers were stuck through the division of the nostrils—there was a blue stone set in her chin—her ear-rings consisted of two pieces of hickery, of the size and shape of drum-sticks—her arms and legs were adorned with bracelets of wampum—her breast glittered with numerous strings of glass beads—she wore a curious pouch, or pocket, of woven grass, elegantly painted with various colours. (195)

In this parodic display of female attire we see traces of contemporary eighteenth-century fashion: certain fashion trends of the 1770s vied with Squinkinacoosta's dress for ridiculousness. Smollett could easily have been thinking of a popular hairstyle from his day: coiffed to towering heights, a lady's hair was decorated with ribbons, feathers, and sometimes even accouterments like animals and miniature ships.[4] In the novel the author means to suggest both the exaggerated parameters of female taste and the fact that this taste, whether it runs to face painting and wampum or very big hair, is both alien and inimical to men. To the male-identified reader, a taste as incomprehensible as that shared by Squinkinacoosta and Tabitha suggests the very otherness at the heart of the female consumer. In an emerging fashion scene that equated preoccupation with dress with women, society decreed that only fops or castrati–men with a questionable sexual orientation–would share Squinkinacoosta's and Tabitha's enthusiasm for self-display.[5]

But female fashion is also more here, for, as the crowning glory, Squinkinacoosta wears around her neck "the fresh scalp of a Mohawk warrior, whom her deceased lover had lately slain in battle." Thus the narrative suggests that

Fashionable Ladies' Hairstyles, 1770s. From *Handbook of English Costume in the Eighteenth Century* (Faber and Faber) *Copyright © the estate of Cecil Willett Cunnington and Phillis Cunnington, 1957*

female adornment requires violent acts of appropriation and that other men pay the gruesome price for female acquisitiveness. Female consumption is a kind of depletion that "eats up" everything in its path, laying waste to what men would otherwise preserve. It becomes symbolically emasculating when it demands the sacrifice of male resources. Thus other female characters, though located in a more "civilized" landscape, also deplete their partners' manhood. The extravagant Mrs. Baynard, for example, lays waste to the phallic trees that once lined the avenues of her husband's ancestral estate (285).

Though Tabitha does not express an enthusiasm for raw flesh, her tastes are as perverted as Squinkinacoosta's. First, her endorsement of Squinkinacoosta's dress as expressing "much taste and fancy" suggests either her indifference to or her tolerance for that lady's most horrific ornament. Then, in the alien environment of the city Tabitha actually prefers the putrid offerings of the city market to the wholesome fare that would have been provided at home, on her brother's estate. Tabitha is like the "fine lady of St. James parish" who admits into her mouth the very cherries that have been cleaned with spittle from the "filthy and, perhaps, ulcerated chaps of a St. Giles huckster" (122). She is as willing to eat any fashionable food, regardless of its corrupted or contaminated state, as she is to pursue the latest trend. All women, the narrator suggests, are perverse in their tastes, driven by foolish, and even dangerous, desires to consume the exotic and the fashionable.[6]

This excerpt from *Humphry Clinker* provides us with an appropriate point of departure for a study of women and consumer culture in eighteenth-century Britain. On the one hand, Smollett's novel only rehearses the older, persistent cultural notion of women as voracious appetite. We can trace this stereotype back through recorded time: feminist anthropologists remind us that women have always been aligned with the body and that historically women's bodies have been troped by synecdoche: mouth and womb have stood in for the female body itself.[7] Plato thought that the womb was the cause of woman's fundamental instability: "In women . . . the womb, a living creature within them with a desire for childbearing, if it be left long unfruitful beyond the due season, is vexed and aggrieved, and wandering throughout the body and blocking the channels of the breath, by forbidding respiration brings the sufferer to extreme distress and causes all manners of disorders."[8] Furthermore, popular wisdom decreed that women had no more control over their mouths than over their wandering wombs. The loose tongue, the propensity toward unlicensed speech or garrulity, was supposedly linked to an unbridled sexuality, as one bodily part doubled for another.[9] Reduced to a giant orifice, a woman's body threatened to take in, to consume with prodigious appetite, but it also threatened to expel, to give monstrous birth to the literal and symbolic progeny that resulted from its appetites. Thus, while the theme of "appetite" pervades Western literary tradition (and not only women have hungry mouths), we could say that, beginning with Eve, *women* with appetites have had a special place in literary and popular lore. Even now culture dictates strong controls over female eating: ladylike portions or slimming diet drinks are signs of an appetite under control, of a woman who has learned to discipline her most unruly impulses to consume everything in sight.[10]

On the other hand, however, Smollett gives us access to a distinctly modern representation of female appetite. Although women's voracity has long been asserted, history awaited the proliferation of consumer commodities to make the specific connection between female appetite and the world of goods. With the birth of a consumer culture, women were assumed to be hungry for *things*—for dresses and furniture, for tea cups and carriages, for all commodities that indulged the body and enhanced physical life. Smollett also provides access to a distinctly modern paradox about female appetite. Though it had been necessary to the strong growth of the expanding British economy, female appetite for goods, by the end of the eighteenth century, was also perceived as a sinister force threatening male control and endangering patriarchal order.

This book aims to explore the presence of Tabitha, as well as other similar representations. Its topic is the ideological construction of the modern female subject in relation to the emerging consumer culture of eighteenth-century Britain. I will argue that, during this period, the female consumer was figured as a powerfully paradoxical presence. She was sometimes depicted as supremely disciplined, at other times as disruptive or disorderly. Society assumed that she could be controlled through disciplinary practices, and it also saw her as threatening male power. She suggested, through the semblance of good behavior, perfect control, yet she also embodied rampant unruliness. Yet these tensions in the female consumer tell us more about the contradictory understanding of emerging consumer behaviors than they do about women themselves. This is a book, then, about how British culture projected onto the female subject both its fondest wishes for the transforming power of consumerism and its deepest anxieties about the corrupting influences of goods.

Over the course of the long eighteenth century, two processes occurred simultaneously. The first was a cultural struggle to define both the meaning of consumption and the practices of modern consumerism. The second was the ideological construction of the female subject. To understand the first is to recognize that the very notion of a *consumer culture* provokes considerable discussion and debate. Distinguished from *commodity culture,* a term derived from a Marxian theory of commodities, consumer culture is often employed by cultural anthropologists, some sociologists, and cultural historians to refer to a range of human investments in, attitudes toward, and behaviors around consumer goods.[11] Though its precise definition varies, depending upon the discipline of the definer, most scholars employing the term hold the basic assumption that, in a modern society, goods carry a wide range of meanings. If, before the modern period, goods already conveyed status, consumer objects became, with the growth of wide-scale consumption, "an expression and guide to social identity." As Grant McCracken explains, "both role differentiation and anonymity were well under way in [the early modern] period and it is likely that goods began to assume this additional semiotic burden. The cultural meaning of goods was increasingly a way an anonymous society could maintain its center."[12]

Historians John Brewer, Neil McKendrick, and Roy Porter provide the rationale for locating the origins of a consumer culture in eighteenth-century Britain. For McKendrick and Brewer, an increased tendency toward "conspicuous consumption"—indeed a veritable "orgy of spending"—marks this period as distinctly modern. This spending, "spurred on by social emulation and class competition," occurred among all the ranks, they assert, and owed its origin to "an unleashing of home demand" as well as to the predominance of London.[13] McCracken reiterates, "Consumption was beginning to take place more often, in more places, under new influences, by new groups, in pursuit of new goods, for new social and cultural purposes."[14] Carole Shammas, Lorna Weatherill, and Beverly Lemire have made this discussion especially relevant to women by exploring particular goods—china, clothing—of importance to them.[15]

Though there have been several incisive critiques of this body of work, it nonetheless seems safe to paint, in broad strokes, the features of early consumer culture.[16] Quite simply, it appears that, in the period from about 1720 on, more goods, of greater variety and improved quality, were available than ever before to a wider range of people. People seem to have expected that certain possessions could be theirs, and those commodities became part of the fabric of their lives. In addition, people appear to have had a different relationship to those goods than previously. They considered objects like furniture or china not merely as useful but also as valuable indication of who and what they were.[17] As I will argue, consumer attitudes about "luxury" changed in relation to evolving notions about "commodiousness." Retail practices also saw a revolution, as buying moved increasingly indoors. A greater variety of commodities was now seen in an enhanced setting, as modern strategies for display and advertising took hold. People now left their homes to encounter a world of goods not in the hands of the pack merchant, or displayed in the open market, but in urban shops and other enclosed retail spaces. The verb *to shop* is, according to the *Oxford English Dictionary*, an eighteenth-century coinage.

Corresponding to these important changes in consumer culture was a widespread debate about the very meaning of consumption. As John Brewer and Roy Porter point out, the word *consume* suggests "both an enlargement through incorporation and a withering away . . . both enrichment and impoverishment."[18] To consume is either to take in what one needs to survive or to waste away in a fit of disease. The noun *consumption* refers not only to a pattern of spending, but to pulmonary tuberculosis. Consumption can entail taking in, swallowing with gluttonous and unstoppable appetite, or it can refer to bodily depletion, a deterioration, and, ultimately, an exhaustion. The pun was not lost on Frances Burney: in *Cecilia* (1782) one character asks another with alarm, "Do you think me ill? Do I look consumptive?" To which Cecilia responds, "Yes, consumptive indeed, but not, I hope, in your constitution."[19] She then councils her friend to retrench her expenses.

For eighteenth-century England, ambiguity in the notion of "consumption" initiated a national debate: should one consider wide-scale consumerism as enhancing the national coffers, allowing for lucrative trade on a global level, or should one recognize that same spending as draining the nation of its capital, rendering it dependent and "weakened" by its inability to live off indigenous resources? In the writings of male writers from the period we see both views at work in the presentation of consumption. What remains constant on either side of the debate, however, is the notion that *women* are the primary consumers. Again and again a society that is deeply ambivalent about its own relationship to consumption focuses its attention on the female body. Writers from both sides of the argument deploy the female body in a debate about the human implications of consumption. On the one hand, the Lady of Fashion (one of the earliest versions of an obsessive shopper) could be perceived as "merely fulfilling the will of God."[20] Her addiction to buying could be justified according to an "economic theodicy" that saw providence as determining human behavior.[21] On the other hand, economic theodicy did not preclude public censure. Moralists like George Berkeley queried "whether a woman of fashion ought not to be declared a public enemy?"[22] The same consumption that fed national coffers when viewed from another angle appeared to be the cause of a country's demise.

For Bernard Mandeville, apologist for a nascent capitalist economy, unbridled consumption was a form of social enrichment. Thus, though he deplored the means women employed to consume, he nonetheless encouraged their spending as necessary to the health of a larger body politic. "It is incredible," he writes in his remarks to *The Fable of the Bees* (1714), "what vast quantity of Trinkets as well as Apparel are purchas'd and used by Women, which they could never have come at by any other means, than pinching their Families, Marketting, and others ways of cheating and pilfring from their Husbands."[23] Without ever questioning the economic arrangement that rendered grown women utterly dependent upon the financial resources of others, Mandeville lists the ways that women finagle what they want out of men. Contemporary readers will recognize stereotypes that have persisted well into the late twentieth century in popular television shows like *Married with Children*:

> [Other women] by ever teazing their Spouses, tire them into Compliance, and conquer even obstinate Churls by their perseverance and their assiduity of asking: A Third sort are outragious at a denial, and by downright Noise and Scolding Bully their tame Fools out of anything they have a mind to; Whilst Thousands by the force of wheedling know how to overcome the best weigh'd Reasons and the most positive reiterated refusals; the Young and Beautiful especially laugh at all remonstrances and denials, and a few of them scruple to Employ the most tender Minutes of Wedlock to promote a sordid Interest.[24]

Still, Mandeville would not have it any other way: without women's "immoral" strategies for gaining what they desire, a capitalist economy could scarcely exist. Mandeville flatters himself that his reader "will be obliged to own, that a considerable Portion of what the Prosperity of *London* and Trade in general, and consequently the Honour, Strength, Safety, and all the Worldly Interest of the Nation, consist in, depends entirely on the Deceit and vile Stratagems of Women."[25] Women's spending, then, is a necessary evil in a consumer society. Mandeville not only essentializes women's consumer behavior, depicting it as the inevitable extension of their otherwise duplicitous nature, he sanctions it.

Writing about Ireland in the 1720s, Jonathan Swift, in contrast, imagines consumption of foreign resources as a depletion, and he projects his anger at Ireland's deplorable economic situation onto women consumers.[26] He argues that women's inordinate predilection for fine, expensive things, only available from abroad, constitutes a significant threat to an Irish national economy—and ultimately to an Irish identity itself. He chastises women for employing "their whole stock of Invention in contriving new arts of profusion, faster than the most parsimonious husband can afford." He complains that "their universal maxim is to despise and detest everything of the growth and manufacture of their own Country, and most to value whatever comes from the very remotest parts of the globe."[27] He claims, "It is absolutely so in fact that every husband of any fortune in the Kingdom is nourishing a poisonous, devouring serpent in his Bosom with all the mischief but with none of its wisdom."[28] If elsewhere he leaves open the possibility that women's education is to blame for this unseemly appetite, he also intimates that women's consumptive impulse is an essential part of their nature. In a homophobic gesture Swift ties the desire for imported luxuries to both a feminine and an effeminate constitution: "It is to gratify the vanity and pride, and luxury of the women, and of the young fops who admire them, that we owe this insupportable grievance of bringing in the instruments of our ruin."[29] Linking patriotism to a strong "masculine identity," to an appreciation for what is homegrown, self-sufficient, and resistant to foreign influence, Swift defines a particular kind of consumerism as antithetical to the national interest. But the mentality of the consumer necessarily partakes of a craving for the novel or the different, the unusual or the exotic: there is no thrill in shopping for what one can obtain at home. Whatever the economic realities of Swift's polemic, it is clear that his portrait of the female Irish consumer functions symbolically. She represents a national restlessness, a turning away from indigenous resources, as well as a vitiated taste to be associated with a weakened constitution. As the "devouring serpent" in the bosom of the kingdom, she becomes the convenient focus for an anger that might have been more productively directed at British colonial exploitation of Irish resources.[30]

I have drawn examples from Smollett, Mandeville, and Swift, three writers who belong to the eighteenth-century canon, to highlight how pervasive and problematic is the theme of the female consumer in the literature of this period. In addition, in the novels of women writers like Frances Burney, Maria Edgeworth, Susan Ferrier, and even Jane Austen, we can detect oblique responses to this theme, representations that both further and refute prevailing cultural assumptions. In Ferrier's *Marriage* (1818), for example, an antiheroine is marked by the psychopathic need to buy. In Burney's *Camilla* (1796) a mere trip to the shops opens up a world of tribulations, which the author shows us from inside the young protagonist's point of view. But in *Sanditon* (1817), Austen's mature heroine, having, we are told, neither

Camilla's youth nor any "intention of her distress," turns wisely from an enticing display of rings and brooches in a shop, choosing only a few modest selections.[31] Though it may indeed be "difficult to imagine one of Jane Austen's heroines . . . endangered by shopping,"[32] the period would have been already familiar with the dangers of a woman's propensity to consume. Several decades later, by the mid-nineteenth century, the department store, with its spectacular display of consumer goods directed at women, would only exacerbate a preexisting, misogynist diatribe about the dangers of undisciplined female desire for material objects.[33]

For the feminist reader who comes to the eighteenth-century canon, these representations constitute a formidable tradition. They say a great deal not only in their explicit text but also in their silence about historical facts. For what *did* motivate women's participation in an eighteenth-century "consumer revolution"? How did women understand their own consumption? Moreover, how do we reconcile their culturally prescribed role as consumers with the fact of their increasing economic disenfranchisement? For the most part, the eighteenth-century canon fails to address such questions. Instead, essentialist assumptions about women—for example, the notion that their "natural" vanity makes them especially susceptible to fashion—have substituted for discussion and analysis.

In response, feminist scholars have, over the last fifteen years, queried the role of eighteenth-century society in the designation of an apparently "natural" femininity. Drawing upon Althusser's notion of an "interpellated subjectivity," they have turned their attention to the ideological process that constructs gender, maintaining that a woman is not born but made.[34] Starting with Mary Poovey's *The Proper Lady and the Woman Writer* (1984), feminist scholars have investigated the multiple discourses responsible for a specific eighteenth-century version of British femininity. Poovey's seminal work on gender was followed by Nancy Armstrong's *Desire and Domestic Fiction* (1987), Kathryrn Shevelow's *Women and Print Culture* (1989), Felicity Nussbaum's *The Autobiographical Subject* (1989), and Laura Brown's *Ends of Empire* (1993).[35] What these works share is the recognition that a gendered subjectivity is produced in relation to other social and economic forces. For all of these writers the *middle-class lady* (the term itself being an anachronism) appeared at a specific moment in Western history to perform a specific cultural function. For Poovey, Armstrong, and Shevelow, in particular, the role of print culture was crucial, as periodicals, conduct manuals, and novels were the media for the expression of a self-conscious, class-bound identity.

In addition, informed by Foucault, a feminist analysis of the period is now alert to the role of the human body in a process of social formation.[36] Observations claimed as biological "fact" about gender (as we noticed in even the most abbreviated history of the female body) are also cultural interpretations, as the human body is appropriated for ideological purposes.[37] The human body, which has no intrinsic meaning, is placed within an economic system that both interprets it and imbues it with meaning. As Foucault writes, "The body becomes a useful force only if it is both a productive body and a subjected body."[38] In eighteenth-century England women's bodies were subjected to a number of disciplinary processes, depending upon class position. It is worth returning to the eighteenth-century context with a Foucauldian reading of the body in order to understand better how those disciplinary processes worked.

This book examines three cultural moments when the dual processes of constructing consumerism and female subjectivity intersected. All three moments–broadly construed as cultural events that gave rise to both textual documentation and shifts in material life–occurred roughly between 1720 and 1820. Seventeen hundred and twenty saw the first flowering of a consumer market and the first appearance of widespread consumer demand for goods like china. Eighteen hundred and twenty brings us to a conventional end of the eighteenth century, the end of the Regency period and movement forward into the Victorian era. By 1820, as well, the second consumer revolution began to take shape in the form of urban shopping centers, arcades, and department stores. But three cultural moments can be said to belong thoroughly to the eighteenth century. They are the development of the tea table, the evolution of retail space and codification of behaviors known as "shopping," and the discursive definition of "business" as male. All three moments brought on an intensified discussion of gender and of what it means to be a woman in particular. Thus an initial set of questions concerning women and consumption leads into more specific issues: how were women's lives altered or changed by cultural discussion of their place at the tea table, in the shop, or in a place of business? What were the consequences of the discursive processes that increasingly placed certain women not at the site of useful employment but in relation to the leisured sites of pleasure? And what about other women whose social positioning precluded their similar placement?

Part 1 addresses three related aspects of the tea table: tea, sugar, and china. The first section focuses on the tea table as a place that makes possible a gendered and class-bound identity. In a range of eighteenth-century texts, from poems by Edmund Waller and William Cowper to polemical treatises by Jonas Hanway and Simon Mason, the tea table becomes the location where the upper-class female body is disciplined to participate in a narcissistic display of availability. At the same time, however, working-class women are warned about the dangers of congregating at the tea table because their bodies are expected to labor for the British economy. Section 2 asks whether female participation in the boycott of Caribbean sugar in the 1790s in fact dissipated the culturally prescribed narcissism of the tea table. Using a key text by a woman writer as my example, I argue that, at the end of the century, the apparently disruptive state of the female body remained an unarticulated obsession with the power to disturb a liberal agenda such as that of the sugar boycott. Section 3 pays special attention to the metaphoric potential of china and explores how this object in particular became a trope for the feminine. In three representative texts by women writers, china is deployed as a marker for an especially superficial construction of femininity. However, I attempt to show how these texts are ideologically motivated. In other words, china allows us to see how society projected its ambivalence about consumer culture onto women.

Part 2, entitled "Shopping," explores the historical specificity of the metaphor "woman as commodity" by examining the evolution of *commodity* and by describing the interior space that emerged as the proper site for selling. Over the course of the century, shopping evolved as an indoor activity. As selling moved indoors, retail practice increasingly relied on interior psychological processes. These processes were conceived in relation to gender, as seller and buyer were placed metaphorically in their respective "masculine" and "feminine" positions. After a reading of gendered activity in three fictional shop scenes, the second section turns to a historical coincidence: modern pornography has been said to emerge at the same moment that first saw the appearance of shopping. In conclusion, the last section explores woman as commodity in relation to this coincidence.

Part 3 takes as its subject the discursive construction of business as masculine. First, in "Businesswomen," drawing on existing historical records, it rehearses the current historical understanding of working women in the business world from the mid-century onward. How can a new historical analysis help us to read these records, and what can such an analysis add to our knowledge of the construction of gender? Discrepancies in historical records on the subject of women's work are not the indication of a "failure to tell the truth"; rather, such gaps are the sign of a nascent gender ideology at work. That ideology was directed at two goals: removal of actual women from the scene of business and the construction of the "feminine" as antithetical to the world of business. Mid-century trade manuals participate in the denigration of both the female and the feminine, as the business world is constructed as a professional, transcendent, and exclusively male. Last, "Prostitutes" turns to the one remaining profession in which both the female *and* the feminine continued to do business, despite all efforts to keep women out of business, namely, prostitution. After a discussion of the bawd as an especially problematic rendering of a businesswoman, the section closes with a paradox: when the female body no longer has a place in business, women's business becomes the body. In texts by writers like George Lillo, Saunders Welch, or Bernard Mandeville women are called upon to do the business of the body—either to bear children or to join the ranks of prostitutes who serve the carnal needs of the business community—once they are no longer allowed access to legitimate business opportunities. In other words, the discursive construction of business as masculine effectively relegates woman to the body. It thereby removes her from the scene of economic opportunity and positions her as the object of consumer society. For if consumption is seen metaphorically as a bodily phenomenon, then woman as body was historically viewed as ready to consume.

I believe there are several advantages to tracing the origins of the female shopper back to eighteenth-century Britain. By focusing on that period, we can attain a clearer sense of how women's "appetite" was diverted toward goods, how shopping became gendered as feminine, and how women's bodies became configured in relation to consumption. In addition, we can obtain an opportunity to "denaturalize" the natural, to ask questions about why *women* shop—in other words, to look at persistent, contemporary cultural stereotypes in new, historically informed, ways. Above all, as feminists we need to resist the notion that consumption is a "bodily" act, for, in truth (as cultural studies teaches us), shopping is much more a state of mind than it is a physical compulsion. Shopping is not just about appetite; it is about projection, fantasy, and desire, among other things. As Mica Nava explains, "Consumerism is far more than just economic activity: it is also about

dreams and consolation, communication and confrontation, image and identity. Like sexuality, it consists of a multiplicity of fragmented and contradictory impulses."[39]

In a recent analysis of postwar, baby-boom women's culture, Susan Douglas testifies to the truth of Nava's assertion:

> When I open *Vogue*, for example, I am simultaneously infuriated and
> seduced, grateful to escape temporarily into a narcissistic paradise
> where I'm the center of the universe, outraged that completely unat-
> tainable standards of wealth and beauty exclude me and most of the
> women I know from the promised land. I adore the materialism; I
> despise the materialism. I yearn for the self-indulgence; I think self-
> indulgence is repellent. I want to look beautiful; I think wanting to
> look beautiful is the most dumb-ass goal you could have. The magazine
> strokes my desire; the magazine triggers my bile. And it doesn't just
> happen when I'm reading *Vogue*; it happens all the time.[40]

Though Douglas's colorful colloquialisms may seem to take us far from our
eighteenth-century context, she articulates well the ambivalence that has
surely been with women consumers since at least 1720. It is almost as if
Smollett's female consumer has been allowed to come to life and defend
herself, two hundred years after her first creation. Rising above the one-
dimensional interior life that her male author gave her, the female consumer
returns to explain the contradictory appeal of consumerism to her inner
sense of herself. She explains how consumer culture enthralls her, yet how
she is able to distance herself critically from the imaginary self it interpel-
lates. Writing in 1994, Douglas captures the profoundly conflicted response
of so many women to consumerism: who has not seen her idealized—and
fictional—self in some similar display, and who has not also performed a
critical act of self-analysis, achieving the same distance from an image
designed to make her lose herself?

The following discussion takes up the challenge to investigate the meaning of consumer culture by returning to the historical origins of some discursive processes and some material practices that brought women into
alignment with consumption. Beginning with the eighteenth-century tea
table as an especially powerful locus for the definition of female subjectivity,
the discussion then turns to two other locations where we are able to trace

the construction of female subjectivity and modern consumer practice—the shop and the business site. All three of these locations belong to the eighteenth century, but they also belong to our own. My purpose in writing this book is to demonstrate that, though history may have modified and altered some of their features, these three locations still exert tremendous influence over our self-definition as women and men.

The Tea Table

Tea

In *Lady Audley's Secret*, by Mary Elizabeth Braddon (1862), the hero pauses to watch the demon lover making tea:

> Surely a pretty woman never looks prettier than when making tea. The most feminine and most domestic of all occupations imparts a magic harmony to her very movement, a witchery to her every glance. The floating mists from the boiling liquid in which she infuses the soothing herbs, whose secrets are known to her alone, envelop her in a cloud of scented vapour, through which she seems a social fairy, weaving potent spells with Gunpowder and Bohea. At the tea table she reigns omnipotent, unapproachable. What do men know of the mysterious beverage? Read how poor Hazlitt made his tea, and shudder at the dreadful barbarism. How clumsily the wretched creatures attempt to assist the witch president of the tea-tray; how hopelessly they hold the kettle, how continually they imperil the frail cups and saucers , or the taper hands of the priestess. To do away with the tea-table is to rob woman of her legitimate empire.[1]

Similarly, in Elizabeth Gaskell's *North and South* (1855) the industrialist, Mr. Thornton, watches with fascination as Margaret Hale makes tea:

She stood by the tea-table in a light coloured muslin gown, which had a good deal of pink about it. She looked as if she was not attending to the conversation, but solely busy with the tea-cups, among which her round ivory hands moved with noiseless daintiness. She had a bracelet on one taper arm, which would fall down over her round wrist. Mr. Thornton watched the replacing of this troublesome ornament with far more attention than he listened to her father. It seemed as if it fascinated him to see her push it up impatiently until it tightened her soft flesh; and then to mark the loosening—the fall. He could almost have exclaimed—"There it goes again!" There was so little to be done after he arrived at the preparation for tea, that he was almost sorry the obligation of eating and drinking came so soon to prevent his watching Margaret.[2]

As I will argue in this chapter, in both of these passages the ritualized behaviors of women at the tea table are the sign of an ongoing process of the disciplining and normalizing of the upper-class female body. That process had come into being in the early decades of the eighteenth century, and it reached its apotheosis in fictionalized nineteenth-century scenes like these.

Both passages convey a series of qualities we are not surprised to find associated with the rituals of the tea table: femininity, delicacy, refinement. Of course, all three are the mark of class and taste. Indeed, Gaskell's Thornton especially notices Margaret's ease at the tea table because it marks her as different from the women of his class. Yet in both scenes such qualities appear in conjunction with the potential disruption of the civilities represented. In the first passage, Hazlitt's "barbarism" at his own tea table only suggests something of the ineptness of all men who "imperil the frail cups and saucers." Above all, Braddon's passage conveys a sense of the precariousness of the tea table: how easily might the magic disappear.

In Gaskell's passage the disruption comes in the form of Thornton's obsessive interest in Margaret's falling bracelet. As the bracelet tightens "her soft flesh," it sends a powerfully charged erotic subtext to Thornton. Gaskell uses the arm, as well as the elaborate choreography of the slipping bracelet, as a metonymy for Margaret's sexuality. The slow descent of the bracelet provokes Thornton's fascination and longing. Then, in a surprise move, Gaskell displaces the erotic subtext between Thornton and Margaret onto a ritualized gesture between Margaret and her father:

> She handed [Thornton] his cup of tea with the proud air of an unwill-
> ing slave; but her eye caught the moment when he was ready for
> another cup; and he almost longed to ask her to do for him what he saw
> her compelled to do for her father, who took her little finger and
> thumb in his masculine hand, and made them serve as sugar-tongs. Mr.
> Thornton saw her beautiful eyes lifted to her father, full of light, half-
> laughter, and half-love, as this bit of pantomime went on between the
> two, unobserved, as they fancied, by any. (74)

Gaskell writes this scene so that Thornton's sense of isolation approximates
our own; like Thornton, we watch Margaret and her father from the outside,
and the scene is structured so that we participate in the male gaze. We, also
like Thornton, do not fully understand the erotic subtext of the daughter's
relation to her father. This subtext, while it disturbs the scene, also enhances
our awareness of ritual.

In the Braddon passage the witch imagery disturbs the surface decorum
and hints at a darker side to the ritual. The tone of the imagery is arguably
aggressive, as if to counter what is "omnipotent" and "unapproachable" in the
lady who reigns over the ceremonies. The mystery of the boiling liquid conflates with the woman's own mysterious powers. The tea becomes a magic
potion, one associated with a metaphysic of fluids. Just as Thornton feels left
out as he watches Margaret, so too does Braddon's male participant. Like
Margaret, Braddon's tea pourer reserves secrets to herself, intimations of an
illicit transgressive life.

I am interested, then, in how these two nineteenth-century scenes manage to evoke a series of conflicting emotions in response to the image of a
woman at the tea table: admiration, envy, fear, isolation, sexual threat, or
loss. As we will see, over the course of the eighteenth century the British
tea table evolved into a place of contrasting meanings. That evolution began
with the cultural definition of the tea table as a gendered site, a "feminine"
locus where the civilizing process could occur. However, in order to participate in the civilizing process, women were required to discipline themselves. The management of female behaviors, gestures, and, above all,
speech, were the prerequisites for women's cultural participation. Yet once
this same paradigmatic construction of femininity began to circulate among
the lower orders, political reaction set in. The female body that was constructed to rule over the tea table was not the female body needed to per-

form England's physical labor. As I will demonstrate, the symbolism of the tea table worked in one direction when the "fluid" female body in question was thought to "leak," or overflow boundaries and in another direction when female fluidity was perceived as a powerful economic resource to be tapped. Thus an examination of tea drinking in eighteenth-century England helps us to see how a particular construction of femininity emerged in relation to a "disciplinary" apparatus (in Foucault's sense of that term).[3] But it also allows us to recognize the important role that class played in that construction.

Tea had been a part of the British scene since the seventeenth century: the first recorded instance of the word *tea* appears in 1615.[4] The first advertisement for tea was in the *Mercurius Politics* in 1658, and Samuel Pepys tasted his first cup two years later.[5] An even more popular product than coffee or chocolate, by the end of the century tea proved to be one of the most lucrative commodities. If in 1700 only twenty thousand pounds were imported, by 1721 tea imports exceeded one million pounds.[6] Between 1721 and 1760 total quantities of tea imported increased by five-fold.[7]

The association of tea with femininity occurs beginning with the marriage of Catherine of Braganza to Charles II. In 1662, in a union designed to shore up an alliance between Portugal and England, on the one hand, and to enhance British coffers, on the other, Catherine came to England as a bride of twenty-three. Her dowry included five hundred pounds sterling, the possession of Tangiers, the rights to free trade with Brazil and the East Indies, and "the island of Bombay."[8] Her marriage thus secured England's preeminent domain over the eastern trading routes and helped to usher in what has been called England's first empire. To commemorate Catherine's role in the expansion of British trade, Edmund Waller wrote, "Of Tea, commended by her Majesty,"[9] in which he acknowledged Catherine and her native Portugal for showing the British the way to "the fair region, where the Sun does rise."

Waller also publicly linked the drinking of tea to the queen. This pronouncement effectively promoted the status of tea as a definitively British, upper-class, feminine, and domestic activity, while implicitly advancing the interests of the East India Trading Company. Tea, claimed Waller, is "the best of herbs"; it aids the fancy because it represses "those vapours which the head invade" and "keeps the palace of the soul serene." The irony of this pronouncement could not be more blatant: unlike the palace of the soul, the literal palace of Charles II was marked by licentiousness, as Charles made public his lack of interest in his dowdy, childless wife.[10]

Despite this irony, the ideological work accomplished by Waller's poem cannot be underestimated. The poem deploys multiple analogies: as the queen is to her tea table, so is any proper British woman to hers. Both "rule" over a site that is simultaneously identified as "civilized" and central to British economic interest. Thus the poem adds to an advancing redefinition of women's cultural contribution.[11] No longer an active economic participant, the proper British lady is accorded two functions: first, to engender decorous and protected domestic space (whatever the sexual practices of one's husband) and, second, to *consume*, to buy not only the tea but also the material effects ensuring the success of the tea table ritual. By 1694 so effectual was the ideological link between women and tea drinking that Mellefont, a character in Congreve's *The Double Dealer*, satirized the ladies as retiring to "tea and scandal, according to their *ancient* custom" (emphasis added).[12]

The history of tea drinking as a domestic private activity parallels the history of coffee drinking. Since Habermas's influential discussion of the bourgeois public sphere, the coffeehouse has been scrutinized for its role in the creation of a bourgeois subject.[13] According to one account, "The late seventeenth-century middle classes welcomed coffee as the great soberer. The coffee drinker's good sense and business efficiency were contrasted with the alcohol drinker's inebriation, incompetence and laziness."[14] The writer elaborates, "Coffee as the beverage of sobriety and coffee as the means of curbing sexual urges—it is not hard to recognize the ideological forces behind this reorientation. Sobriety and abstinence have always been the battle cry of puritanical, ascetic movements."[15]

In Stallybrass and White's account, the coffeehouse played a vital role in the disciplining of the male bourgeois body by providing "a radically new kind of social space, at once free from the 'grotesque bodies' of the alehouse and yet (initially at least) democratically accessible to all kinds of men— though not, significantly, to women." In other words, the coffeehouse became "an important instrument in the regulation of the body, manners and morals of its clientele in the public sphere."[16] Describing how certain forms of behavior, in particular a norm of sobriety, became associated with the coffeehouse, Stallybrass and White explain,

The coffee-house was one of the places in which *the space of discourse was being systematically decathected.* Intoxication, rhythmic and unpredictable movements, sexual reference and symbolism, singing and chanting, bodily pleasures and 'fooling around,' all these were prohibited in the coffee-house. The emergence of the public sphere required that its spaces of discourse be *de-libidinized* in the interests of serious, productive and *rational* intercourse.[17]

However, while the male body was being subjected to its own disciplining process, while it was, in a sense, being rendered "more masculine" in the coffeehouse, a corresponding process was taking place in relation to the tea table. There, through a similar emphasis on the disciplining of the body, one became more "feminine."[18]

In *Poem in Praise of Tea* Peter Motteux offers one depiction of the feminizing process thought to occur at the tea table.[19] First, though, he makes obvious his particular investment in the subject of the tea table. He identifies himself as one "engrost" by "my CHINA and INDIAN trade, and all the distracting Variety of a Doyly, and ready to cross the seas again to Recruit those new branches of Foreign Silks, Lace, Linens, Pictures, and Other Goods." Little wonder, then, that Motteux should so praise the salutary effects of one of his own commodities. His description of the effects of tea upon the wine drinker suggests how notions about gender could be employed to sell a product. Explaining the benefits of tea, Motteux writes,

> I drink and the kindly streams arise,
> Wine's Vapour flags, and soon subsides and dies.
> The friendly Spirits brighten mine again,
> Repel the Brute, and re-inthrone the Man.
> The rising Charmer with a Pleasing Ray
> Dawns on the Mind, introduces Day.
> So its parent with presenting Light,
> Recalls Distinction, and displaces Night.

Motteux's description makes tea quite literally the drink of the Enlightenment, as it is the substance that banishes the darkness of wine and the forces associated with it, in particular, brutishness and animalistic behavior. In his account tea both humanizes and civilizes; it saves the British gentleman who would otherwise remain in his drunken stupor. What is more, Motteux's verse echoes Waller's: both praise tea as an antidote to those "vapours" raised by wine. When a British gentlewoman serves this tea, she also participates in this process of enlightenment, refinement, and civilization. Motteux's choice of the phrase "rising Charmer" for tea suggests he has in mind some metonymic connection between woman and the substance she employs to domesticate her man. Both tea and woman "act upon" the man in need of humanizing, and tea stands only as a partial representation of a larger feminizing and civilizing force at work in British culture.

However, while both men and women could be "feminized" at the tea table, that process had special ramifications for the female subject, whose identity was shaped more often in relation to this space. To begin, cultural patterns that have historically placed women at the site of food preparation made their place at the tea table seem "natural." Tea was most often served by the mistress of the house, by the eldest daughter, or by the youngest married woman in the group.[20] As in any other food ritual, "repetitiveness serve[d] the meaning being expressed."[21] Gestures, often organized to show off an expensive tea equipage to its full advantage, were to be predictable and organized. The correct placement of a spoon carried significance, while other facets of the tea ceremony—the placement of the guests themselves, the handing round of cups, and so forth—also conveyed meaning.[22]

If, as anthropologist Sherry Ortner explains, the transformation of the "raw" into the "cooked" marks the transition from nature to culture, then women's participation in the tea ceremony further symbolizes her movement from the realm of the natural to the cultural.[23] And on another level (as we will see in greater detail later) the semiotic association of tea as fluid or liquid ensured a connection between tea drinking and the female body, which has also been culturally encoded as "fluid." Thus the notion of the tea table as a feminizing locus was enhanced by essentialized understanding of the female body. To drink tea in the presence of a lady—whose own fluid "essence" was never far from the surface—was to participate symbolically in the triumph of form over nature.

However, this triumph of form only occurs once the body at the tea table has been thoroughly disciplined. Foucault posits some means by which the body was made "docile" over the course of the eighteenth century. His examples—among them creating a sense of "rhythm," correlating body and ges-

"A Family Being Served Tea," c. 1740–1745, British school. *Courtesy of the Yale Center for British Art, Paul Mellon Collection*

tures, breaking down bodily movements into their smallest components— come from a military, industrial, medical, or academic setting. But his insights work equally well for the tea table: there an intense scrutiny given to the smallest gesture suggests a disciplinary apparatus being applied to the female body. As a "calculated manipulation of its elements, its gesture, its behaviors," the tea ritual was also one manifestation of "a machinery of power" exploring, breaking down, and rearranging the upper-class female body.[24] In this instance the particular curve of the wrist as it holds a cup of tea or a modest bend in the neck as the sugar is stirred suggest docility. Again, it is important to note that this particular disciplinary apparatus is entirely class-bound: the same gestures in a serving maid or cook would seem not only ridiculous but also as potentially threatening to a codified class structure.[25]

Another important element of the Foucauldian disciplinary apparatus is the panopticon, the notion that the individual "is seen, but he does not see; he is the object of information, but never a subject in communication" (200). Eighteenth-century publications like the *Tatler* and the *Spectator* offer one version of the panoptic gaze operating on female subjectivity. While a dis-

embodied voice sees the female body, commenting on its excesses, pre-
scribing correctives, the female subject herself does not return the gaze.
Instead, she is often represented as turning her attention to the world of
goods. Steele's narrator, for example, takes special pleasure in viewing "the
finest Laces held up by the fairest Hands; and there examined by the beauteous Eyes of the Buyers the most delicate Cambricks, Muslins, and Lin-
nens."[26] Synecdochically represented as Hands and Eyes, these are fragments
of the women who preside over the tea table. Their "Fairest Hands" speak of
a life free from labor, while their "Beauteous Eyes" reflect the material goods
that mark the purchaser's status. In this way the panoptic voice of eighteenth-century journalism normalizes the upper-class woman to participate
in a narcissistic display.

For William Cowper, as for Peter Motteux, the tea table affords the
opportunity for a respite from the "brutish" side of manhood. Unlike Motteux, however, Cowper also plays on the difference between the "inside" and
the "outside," making the site of the tea table a fortress against the world.
Book 4 of "The Task"[27] describes what is arguably the quintessential domestic scene:

> Now stir the fire, and close the shutters fast,
> Let fall the curtains, wheel the sofa round,
> And, while the bubbling and loud-hissing urn
> Throws up a steamy column, and the cups,
> That cheer but not inebriate, wait on each,
> So let us welcome peaceful ev'ning in.

Recognizable by now is the opposition between the clarity of mind brought
on by the drinking of tea and the inebriation brought on by wine. Here that
clarity of mind is most conducive to the reading of the newspaper, an activity described at length in the lines that follow. What Cowper's description
recreates well is, of course, the sense of coziness, of the familiar (with all its
allusion to *family*), of being safely protected and isolated from the world of
men and men's business. Domesticity reigns, yet no human person—and
certainly no particular woman—is described as responsible for its implementation. An unidentified being, spoken to through the direct address, stirs
the fire, closes the curtains, wheels the sofa round. Metonymy replaces
agency: *cups* wait.

In the lines that follow, Cowper goes on to describe the world antithetical to the scene at the tea table:

> Not such his ev'ning, who with shining face
> Sweats in the crowded theatre, and, squeez'd
> And bor'd with elbow-points through both his sides,
> Out-scolds the ranting actor on the stage:
> Nor his, who patient stands till his feet throb,
> And his head thumps, to feed upon the breath
> Of patriots, bursting with heroic rage,
> Or placemen, all tranquillity and smiles.

This is a world to which no respectable woman might have access; it is the world the respectable woman pouring tea has the power to make vanish. Only once does Cowper explicitly evoke the presence of any specific women. He describes them as "the fair, / Though eloquent themselves" who fear to break the silence of his reading. Yet despite the curious absence of female bodies, this scene resembles what is culturally encoded as the "feminine": here one experiences the events of the world vicariously, never engaging directly in any action, but only imagining what it might be like to participate in the world:

> 'Tis pleasant through the loop-holes of retreat
> To peep at such a world; to see the stir
> Of the great Babel, and not feel the crowd;
> To hear the roar she sends through all her gates
> At a safe distance, where the dying sound
> Falls a soft murmur on th'uninjur'd ear.

It is, of course, the speaker's male privilege to reject this cacophonous scene, to choose the sanctuary of the silent "fair" over the noise of the crowd. In an interesting move, Cowper personifies Babel as female, attributing to her both the "crowd," masses of undisciplined bodies, and the "roar," the powerful noise that issues from those bodies—perhaps in keeping with biblical allusions that identity Babel as a place of excessive language. The oppositions in this poem initially appear as home versus world, inside versus outside, feminine versus masculine, quiet or silent versus noisy. And yet the noise of the female-personified city problematizes the silence of the refined, bodiless lady whose presence the scene evokes. Banished from the inside, the disruptive potential of a body imagistically identified as female shows up on the outside. The very existence of Babel as a place to be viewed through the loophole or an opening in the fortification compromises Cowper's alignment of the female with the feminine and the domestic: what is to prevent the woman on the inside from joining the crowd on the outside? What is to prevent her unexpressed eloquence from erupting into a "roar"?

In the passages we have seen so far, the tea table has emerged as a feminized location, a site associated with women, where certain kinds of brutish or animalistic behaviors have been sublimated in favor of decorous restraint. Both men and women are "feminized" by contact with the tea table, but that process has a different valence for each gender. In each case the feminizing process said to occur at the tea table also signals privilege and marks class distinction. In order to experience the pleasures of the tea table as described by Motteux or Cowper, one must certainly have leisure as well as a high standard of material wealth. In this opportunity for conspicuous consumption the upper-class woman herself becomes a item of display at the tea table: she herself becomes part of the equipage; the narcissistic display of her body becomes part of the ceremony.

The female body could also be broken down into smaller pieces, as one historical anecdote suggests: women of the 1770s bleached their hands with arsenic in order to produce a dazzling effect. The potter Wedgwood responded by producing black teapots to enhance the whiteness of the hands.[28] What is at work, then, is the kind of metonymic displacement we saw in Gaskell: white hands on a tasteful black teapot become the sign of sexual availability within class parameters. Whiteness becomes the signal that a woman exists within a leisured sphere, where she never labors, where her body never sweats or becomes otherwise sullied. The woman with white hands exists, rather, to facilitate male pleasure. In its reciprocal blackness, the teapot establishes a complementarity between the woman and the items on the tea table. Indeed, in the Gaskell passage the woman's body actually comes to substitute for the items on the table, as Margaret's father uses her fingers as the sugar tongs.

Given this emphasis on the narcissistic display of the upper-class female body, it is interesting that for both Motteux and Cowper the feminizing experience of the tea table does not necessarily depend upon the presence of real women. In Cowper's poem, in particular, female bodies are unobtrusive almost to the point of disappearing from the room. The women make no sound, while Babel is displaced to the streets. Noise—and female noise in particular—should have no place in the civilizing process, and the tea table also emerges as a place where female speech must be controlled.

However, while women's gestures were easily regulated, female speech was more difficult to discipline. A number of writers—both male and female—write of the tea table as a place where women's conversation runs scandalously free. For example, in a work entitled *The Tea-Table, or A Conversation* Eliza Haywood describes the upper-class tea table as the place where the curious "inform themselves of the Intrigues of the Town": "In fine, is there any Irregularity in Conduct, any Indecorum in Behavior or Dress, any Defect in Beauty, which is not fully expiated on [at the tea table]?—Scandal, and Ridicule seem here to reign with uncontented sway, but rarely suffer the intrusion of any other themes."[29] Similarly, Edward Young writes of the vicious behavior of women who gather at the tea table:

> Tea! how I tremble at thy fatal stream!
> As Lethe, dreadful to the love of fame!
> What devastations on thy banks are seen!
> What shades of mighty names which once have been!
> An hecatomb of characters supplies
> Thy painted altar's daily sacrifice.
> H–, P–, B–, aspers'd by thee, decay,
> As grains of finest sugars melt away,
> And recommend thee more to mortal taste:
> Scandal's the sweet'ner of a female feast.[30]

With its recourse to the mock heroic, Young's satire envisions a world of destructive female capacity. In this misogynist poem, instead of nurturing and supporting each other (or their husbands or children, for that matter), women are concerned only with social competition. As a "fatal stream," tea is a substance that brings women together, but it also substitutes metaphorically for female fluidity. What spills out here are those very sinister qualities thought to reside in the female character.

Within the context cited by Haywood or Young, it is impossible that women should use the occasion of their assembly to do anything constructive. This is not the splendid colloquy celebrated, for example, by Hannah More in her poem "Bas Bleu, Or the Conversation," but, according to Young's or Haywood's depiction, the most unpleasant kind of gossip. Yet insistence on the viciousness of women's speech suggests a phobic reaction. What is revealed is an anxiety about the power of women's words. Women's speech, when its operates beyond the bounds of a disciplinary apparatus, has the power to bring on death and destruction.

Though women's speech was always viewed as threatening, the conversation of lower-class women at the tea table unleashed its own polemic. This polemic occurred in response to a very different image of the laboring female body. Unlike her upper-class counterpart, the working woman was never encouraged to dally at the tea table, and she was warned against narcissistic self-display. The body of the upper-class woman was disciplined to facilitate male pleasure; the body of the working woman was formed to labor for England. If for the upper-class woman the pressing issue was containment of fluidity, for the laboring woman the issue was the *proper direction* of her fluidity. In essays such as Jonas Hanway's "An Essay on Tea" or Simon Mason's *The Good and Bad Effects of Tea Considered* the body of the laboring-class woman, far from being sublimated, is called forth as a physical entity, as a liquid resource to be tapped for the British national economy. First, though, how did Hanway see tea itself?

What had pleased Peter Motteux about the tea table, namely, its association with a feminizing process, is precisely what worried Hanway.[31] In "An Essay on Tea" (published in the second volume of a book entitled *A Journal of Eight Days Journey*),[32] Hanway begins by refuting the argument for the salutary effects of tea. "This custom of sipping warm liquors affords a gratification, which becomes so habitual, as hardly to be refined. It has prevailed over a great part of the world; some of the most effeminate people on the face of the whole earth, whose example we, as a wise, active, and warlike nation, would least desire to imitate, are the greatest sippers" (17). To make his point still more explicit, Hanway adds, "I mean the Chinese, among whom the first ranks of people, though they exercise themselves with the bow and arrow, have adapted it as a kind of principle to prefer any labour or useful office of life: and yet, with regard to the custom of sipping tea, we seem to act more wantonly and absurdly than even the Chinese" (17).

Hanway has a specific polemic: to ensure the building of a strong army for England's defense.[33] According to his logic, tea is at the root of England's military weakness. As he writes, "What an army have gin and tea destroyed!" (89). Tea literally and metaphorically works against the building of a strong military state. Literally, tea is a drain on British economy: gold and silver leave England in payment for the huge amounts of tea consumed by the British public. "The stress of my argument," writes Hanway, "is laid upon the *consumption of tea*, as an article which *drains* us, most *unprofitably*, of our gold and silver" (173). Like other luxurious imported products—silk, in particular—tea upsets the balance of trade.[34] Hanway argues that money spent on the importing of tea ought to be spent on improving the country instead (189).[35] But this insistence on tea as a literal drain on the British economy depends heavily upon the idea of tea as a substance that metaphorically robs or depletes England of its "vital" and "precious" substances. Excessive importing is, in this sense, a vitiating activity, one that drains England of what it needs in order to be "wise, active, and warlike." If the state is gendered as male, then drinking imported tea emasculates it, renders it impotent.[36]

In an earlier text, which Hanway perhaps read in translation, Simon Pauli compared the practice of drinking tea to a venesection, a blood letting or bleeding, and he similarly urged Western men to avoid drinking foreign imported substances: "I attempt to preserve all Europe by persuading its Inhabitants not to exchange our salutary Regimen for that of the Asiatics and Chinese by following their custom of drinking tea."[37] Even Dr. Johnson, despite some avowed differences of opinion with Hanway on the effects of tea, agreed that tea drinking weakens a strong, muscular constitution: "Tea is one of the stated amusements of the idle and luxurious. The whole mode of life is changed, every kind of voluntary labor, every exercise that strengthened the nerves and the muscle, is fallen into disuse."[38] Though Johnson shifts his emphasis from the product to the lifestyle associated with it, his argument too suggests a concern with the vitiating effects of tea: England loses something of its manly vitality when it succumbs to the affectations associated with tea drinking.

The sense of tea as a draining substance is enhanced by one of Hanway's lengthier digressions into the state of English nurses. Here we see how the tea table elicited public discussion about the proper direction of the working woman's fluidity. Echoing a common concern with the high mortality rate, particularly among wet-nursed children,[39] Hanway blames tea drinking for England's lack of military preparedness. "If we are to be a free people," he writes, "we must be in a capacity to defend ourselves" (55). The working poor are essential to this goal, as they will furnish the 120,000 men necessary for war (50). But the wet nurses who are to raise this future army are spending their money on tea rather than on nutritious food. As a result, their milk is inadequate and the children they raise are weakly or sickly or they die. Hanway is certain that the effect of the nurses' drinking hot liquids is not salutary, and he places a pig's tail in boiling water to prove his point (an experiment that Dr. Johnson later ridiculed in his review of the book). He argues that hot tea is a "liquid fire," which extinguishes that "Promethean fire" in the breast milk "no liquid fire can ever restore again" (109). He further attacks the nurse's tea drinking as the center of her dissipated lifestyle, one erroneously spent in the pursuit of luxury; "Luxury has introduced an artificial appetite, which must needs make great havoc amongst mankind" (64).

Here Hanway makes a series of rapid connections worth pausing over. First, the concern with the poor nutrition of the nursing woman is not unreasonable. Later in the century John Lettsom also described the malnutrition that resulted when scarce family resources went for the purchase of expensive tea: "These effects [of malnutrition] are not to be attributed so much to the peculiar properties of this costly vegetable, as to the want of proper food, which the expense of the [tea] deprived these poor people from procuring."[40] Similarly, Eliza Haywood's *Female Spectator* describes how tea drinking disrupts familial economy and perverts female taste. John Careful writes in to complain of the tradesman's wife whose life is consumed by her passion for tea: "The tea table, as managed in some families, costs more to support than would maintain two children at Nurse. Yet is this by much the Least Part of the Evil; it is the utter Destruction of all Oeconomy—the Bane of good housewifery—and the Source of Idleness, by engrossing those Hours which ought to be employed in honest and prudent Endeavor to add to, or preserve what Fortune, or former Industry has bestowed."[41] Writing as the editor, Haywood shares John Careful's viewpoint: "But alas! The Passion we have for exotics [like Tea] discovers itself but in too many instances, and we neglect the Use of what we have within ourselves, for the same Reason as some Men do their wives, only because they are their own" (101).

Nonetheless, the concern with the nursing woman's health does not entirely explain away this rhetoric, for a double standard operates here. If tea is an unsalutary substance, then proper ladies should have also been warned away from it. But Hanway's polemic against nursing women works with a very different concept of the female body. Exempt from the civilizing mission attributed to her upper-class sister, the nursing woman at the tea table is not invisible or bodiless. Her body is foregrounded precisely because of its productive value. Her liquid assets are not to be contained but to be channeled back into England's coffers. This occurs when her milk nurtures future British citizens or when other aspects of her physicality are deployed. But, in either case, the appetite for tea is dangerous because it interferes with the proper direction of her physical capacity. While pro-tea discourse refined the female body nearly out of existence, reducing it to a highly ritualized series of gestures, anti-tea discourse reintroduces that same female body as a potential locus of control, a place to be "colonized," in Ruth Perry's sense of that word.[42] What makes this "colonization" possible is the fact of concrete physical effects—mother's milk and (as we shall see later in a discussion of the sugar boycott) blood itself.

That working women proved resistant to this control is obvious from the tenor of additional polemics on the subject of tea drinking. For instance, Simon Mason, in *The Good and Bad Effects of Tea Considered*,[43] distinguishes upper-class use of tea from lower-class use. For the upper classes, regardless of gender, tea may well have positive medical benefits. For example, people who have eaten a luxurious supper the night before should drink strong tea at breakfast to "cleanse the stomach, allay the Throat, [and] to comfort and brace up the relaxed state of the Fibres" (28). In addition, tea drinking may be conducive to good conversation—provided, of course, that the tea is not followed by a dram. But Mason is vehement in his objection to the lower orders, or working classes, who imitate their betters, wasting not only their money but their time. As he begins his polemic, his tea drinker becomes gendered as female; he seems to imagine that only working *women* drink tea.

His chief complaint is that drinking tea encourages the working woman to neglect her family:

> I beg the Women's Pardon, for amongst the lower Set, the Men are excluded to partake, if at Home, tho' perhaps they are labouring at the Anvil, the Plough, or carrying a Hod of Mortar, when their Wives are regaling with their Tea, and some bad Spirits they can best come at. These poor Creatures, to be fashionable and imitate their Superiors, are neglecting their Spinning, Knitting, and etc. spending what their Husbands are working hard for; their Children are in Rags, gnawing a

brown Crust, while these Gossips are canvassing over the Affairs of the whole Town, making free with the good Name and Reputation of their Superiors, vilifying and reproaching those a little more reserved than themselves because they have not entered the List.

The women Mason describes here have failed to be productive. The words they "spend" so freely stand in for family resources: it is because these women extravagantly spend words that their children are hungry. Rather than using their bodies to produce cloth—or healthy children—these women are engaging in idle gossip eventually leading to social insubordination. They have not been properly disciplined within the home economy.

Moreover, worse still for Mason is the fact that drinking tea disrupts the sexual status quo among the lower orders. In short, he writes,

> Tea-drinking and etc. in an Afternoon, especially amongst the lower Sort, has impoverished many Families; not only from the Expense altogether, but by idle gossiping Meetings, which abound with Scandal, Reproach, Backbiting, and ill Advice; the Minds of too many vitiated and allured, to imitate evil Practices, occasion Discord, and prevent that quiet Harmony which ought to subsist between Man and Wife" (46).

In a detailed passage Mason describes a world "turned upside down," one in which women have seized the initiative and conspire to emasculate men by stripping them of their power. I cite at length to convey the tone of Mason's comment. Here he describes how the wife, pleased with the effect of a first cup of tea, takes up a second,

> till wound up into a proper Pitch to join in idle Prattle, till a piece of Reproach or Scandal is advanced, concerning some Neighbor, whose wife hath been too free with such a certain Man: Then praise another Man of quiet Disposition and great Humility, who behaves with utmost Submission, and hath lately bought his wife a fine gown and etc. Another, who, for Peace and Quietness, tamely submits to all his Dame directs; works hard, and never goes out to an Ale-house to spend Two-pence, and etc. Others, who are not so Spaniel-bred, as these good Women call it, rebel, and will not go of their Errands, while she tips another Man a Favour; upon which they often combat; he, not willing

to be beat, turns about in a Light, that Man is a cruel Fellow, beats his Wife, and all that is bad. (44)

As Mason describes them, these tea-drinking women of the lower orders are metaphorically rendering their husbands impotent: through their talk they seek to cultivate husbands, who are tame, submissive, meekly generous, obedient to their wives' every whim, and completely economically accountable. These are strong women who assume the upper hand (or at least pretend to do so) and who enjoy the idea of sexual freedom while duping their spouses. Their chief weapon in this war of the sexes is their words, the idle chatter brought on by the drinking of tea together: "Well, then, at one of these Meetings all the Fault is laid upon the Man, and Ways and Means consulted, how to subdue him; for, say they, should we once suffer an Instance of this Kind to be known, we shall have them rebel, and be refractory, and they will take upon them to be Masters" (44).

His emphasis on the destructive power of female speech brings us back to a very old misogynist stereotype, one that we have already seen at work in Edward Young, among others, but, in context, the speech of the working woman is most important as a sign of her ongoing resistance to the subordination Mason seeks. Through her conversation at the tea table, the working woman resists the control Mason wishes to place upon her bodily movements. In talking, she resists a patriarchal hierarchy as well as male economic and sexual control. Even though her rebellion operates only within her circle, it nonetheless suggests the subversive power of women's speech across class lines: women's voice retains the power to subvert discipline, to speak audibly of needs and desires. The ultimate irony, then, is that the tea table, which had been imagined as a locus of control and discipline, as "feminizing" space where the "brutish" might be sublimated, as well as a place from which the "noisy" might be banned, should become precisely the opposite when appropriated by working women.

In the next section we will see how cultural obsession with the fluid nature of the female body further compromised the tea table as a controlling site. As long as women's bodies were perceived in relation to fluidity, the possibility of female subversion persisted. Even when women disciplined themselves, what erupted was the apparently irrepressible nature of the female character. As public attention shifted from milk to blood, women were perceived in relation to the moral corruptions of consumption.

Sugar

Let us pause to reconsider two very different portraits of a lady. The first—familiar to us from the tea discussion—sits gracefully at the tea table. Her white hands hold, in a carefully choreographed gesture, a black teapot designed by Josiah Wedgwood to enhance the paleness of her skin. The second lady also sits at the tea table. Seen now in full figure, she ornaments her body with a medallion also designed by Wedgwood. It depicts (in the words of the connoisseur) "a finely modeled supplicating negro slave in black on a cane colored ground with the impressed inscription 'AM I NOT A MAN AND A BROTHER?' filled in with black."[1] Whether the medallion is worn as broach or bracelet, earring or hair ornament, it signals her sympathy with the abolition movement. Worn at the tea table, it may well indicate that she has decided to boycott Caribbean sugar, the most notorious product of slave exploitation.

My question is how to read the first portrait against the second. Initially, the two figures would seem to reverse each other. The first lady, represented metonymically by white on black, is countered by the second who wears black on white: one historian describes how the image on the medallion "anatomizes the humanity of its subject while dramatizing its black skin."[2] The first figure epitomizes a particular eighteenth-century discursive construction of femininity: as object of display, as focus for the male gaze. The second figure deflects attention away from herself in favor of her cause.

"Slave Medallion," Josiah Wedgwood. *Courtesy of the Trustees of the Wedgwood Museum, Barlaston, Staffordshire, England*

The male gaze is meant to linger on the figure of her medallion, to move beyond the woman herself to larger, more humanitarian concerns. The second figure, then, offers a competing discursive construction of femininity, one that also arises in relation to the tea table, and it serves a different purpose.

Or does it? Does the narcissism that is so thoroughly a feature of the first portrait disappear with the second? Perhaps, instead, when the medallion is worn to ornament a woman's figure, it focuses the male gaze not on the black male slave whose story it tells but on the body of the woman who wears it. What the viewer sees is evidence of a deeper, more "humanitarian" female subjectivity that attracts and fixates even greater attention. As I will argue, the culturally prescribed narcissism of the tea table does not necessarily disappear in the moment when the tea drinker expresses her sympathy with the cause of the black slave by boycotting sugar; rather, it can reappear in other, more problematic and diffuse forms.

The concern, then, is how a late eighteenth-century, liberal political discourse against slavery, though motivated by genuine sympathy and altruism, was compromised by a particular discursive construction of femininity. As I will show, white, liberal women writers, no doubt prompted by moralistic concern for black slaves, were nonetheless compelled to return to the white female body as their subject. Working against a powerful discursive construction of woman herself as other, as a fluid and "dark" force beyond social control, the female abolitionist inevitably displaced her own normalizing narrative onto the body of the black slave.

Let us return to the first lady. Her hands are white because she never works; to the contrary, by social definition, her purpose is to live off the resources and labor of others. In addition, her "essential" nature is troped by the liquids of the tea table. As we have seen, tea, a "feminizing" substance, is her particular drink. Both tea and the female tea drinker are thought to "civilize" what is essentially brutish in men. But, on an even broader level, liquid tea is the appropriate emblem for femininity, since historically the female body has been represented in relation to fluidity, liquidity, and water. As Cixous writes, woman "belongs to the race of waves."[3]

According to Ruth Salvaggio, during the Enlightenment the perceived instability of the female body was believed to be rooted in a fluid female anatomy: "Although the old myth that hysteria was caused by the displacement and movement of the womb was largely rejected [in the eighteenth century], physicians nonetheless believed that the uterus and womb effected hysteria through a diffusion of humors and nerves." Thus Enlightenment culture continued to link woman's "fluid instability" to her madness. "Fluidity, we might say," writes Salvaggio, "has come to be associated with the threat of woman as other—the danger of a potentially controlled dispersion that cannot be fixed in place, that seeps through 'the cracks in the overall system.' "[4] Hence the particular power of the symbolism of the tea table, where nothing "leaks," where the stream of liquid is carefully mastered and ceremoniously controlled.[5] In presenting to others a delicate cup of tea, a woman metaphorically presents an image of her own "essential nature." She indicates that her own female sexuality has been tamed, rendered innocuous. Only when she is "out of control" does the cup break, the table tip, the liquid spill. Hogarth illustrates just such a moment in the second plate of "The Harlot's Progress," where the harlot's demise is signaled by her upsetting the tea table with her foot. Hogarth uses shattered china to denote her shattered virtue; as the tea pot hits the ground, it will spill out its liquid, just as the harlot's excessive sexuality "spills out of" her body. Indeed, one wanton breast has already begun to

Plate 2 from *The Harlot's Progress* by William Hogarth. *Courtesy of the print collection of the Lewis Walpole Library, Yale University*

appear from the top of her dress, while everyone in her presence looks on in mute horror.

When the tea is sweetened with sugar, further semiotic meanings arise. From the earliest days of its availability, women were assumed to have a special fondness for the sweet substance. Dr. Frederick Slare, for instance, assumed that, "not being debauch'd by sowre or uncouth Drama, or offensive Smoak, or the more sordid juice of the Indian Henbane, which is Tobacco," women would naturally prefer sugar.[6] Slare projected that women would form a prime market for sugar. Slare's argument was advanced, no doubt, by the special place that sweetness has always had in a lexicon of femininity. Often associated with human sexuality, sugar has been (and continues to be) an especially potent metaphor for the *female* body. Writing on the curious connection between physical love and sweetness (where salt seems the more appropriate taste), Sidney Mintz notes that "only one liquid product of the human body tastes unmistakably sweet, and that is mother's milk."[7] Though Mintz dismisses the association, there does seem to be some connection, on a psychoanalytic level, between infantile memory and the projection of sweetness onto the female form.

Thus the woman who refuses to eat sugar accomplishes several purposes. First, she breaks the economic chain that makes her the intended receiver of the product of everyone else's labor. She boycotts not only a product but also a cultural construction of herself as an unconscionable consumer, as an unscrupulous appetite. She demonstrates that she is not narcissistically poised, waiting for the world to be laid at her feet. In addition, she breaks the semiotic chain that aligns her with the very properties of sugar itself. Refusing to imbibe sweeteners, she indicates she is not all "sweetness," that she is not to be associated with mindless sensual pleasures.

Still, scholars interpret the participation of white women in the sugar boycotts of the 1790s in different ways. On the one hand, Moira Ferguson reads this particular aspect of women's political activism as a part of a larger liberal agenda. Through identification with the oppression of others, she argues, white women helped to advance a discourse of rights:

> Though constituted unsystematically, [the writing of women partici-
> pating in the sugar boycott] helped to dismantle the blanket of objec-
> tification of Africans and African-Caribbean slaves. They accomplished
> this mediation of othering by being closer in spirit and everyday expe-
> rience to the lot of the disadvantaged. With a personally vested inter-
> est in attacking tyranny that accompanied a sense of themselves as pub-
> lic spokeswomen, they tended less to view slaves within the discrete
> category of simple, familiar charity cases.[8]

In a similar vein, Clare Midgley argues for a fuller understanding of women's participation in popular antislavery mobilizations. "Abstention [from sugar] was seen from the first as a particularly female concern, and it provided women with another important opportunity to actively participate in the abolition campaign," she asserts. If women had been denied an active part as petitioners, the sugar boycott "exposed their power as domestic consumers to have a direct effect on commerce and an indirect influence on politics."[9]

From a postcolonial perspective, on the other hand, the issues become more complicated, as the same language that promotes a liberal cause can prove complicitious in racist discourse. According to Deirdre Coleman, for example, "the ideology of anti-slavery is closely allied to that of colonization and imperialism."[10] In Charlotte Sussman's analysis the notion of "abstention" is tied to a potentially racist discourse of "blood." In other words, "abstention from colonial products might work to purify the domestic space, to purge the domestic body of the racial contamination of African blood, sweat and tears." Thus, "women's political power . . . lay in their ability to regulate the domestic space, keeping its contents separate from the economic dynamics of colonial trade."[11]

The stakes, then, are very different in these two interpretations of women's participation in the sugar boycott. The first, the "liberal" reading, identifies a progressive political agenda—the gradual recognition of black subjectivity—while the second, "postcolonial" approach discovers a nearly phobic urge to isolate an expressly racial interest. Postcolonial critics like Coleman or Sussman isolate the metaphors of contamination that permeate the antisugar discourse, and they focus on the notion of cannibalism to suggest how cultural boundaries were conceived along racial lines.

Certainly, there is some truth to both interpretations: to identify a racist discourse at the heart of a liberal agenda is not necessarily to discredit the Western liberal tradition that ultimately brought the abolition of the slave trade and advanced a discourse of rights. Yet a powerful fact remains: in literature from both sides of the sugar debate, sentiments about contamination and purification, eating and not eating are complicated by patterns of imagery that apply equally well to the *slave's* body and the *woman's* body. Images of blood and milk, used most often to represent sugar, refer the reader not only to the slave's body but back to the female body as well. Thus the debate over sugar implicitly raises the question whether the "contamination" of colonialism comes from the inside or the outside. Are colonial products, which "corrupt" British tastes by infiltrating British blood, the source of contamination, or does the origin of contamination lie within a gendered body that cannot control its insatiable appetite in the first place? For women writers in particular this question exists as an urgent, unarticulated agenda. Abstention from slaves' "flesh" as sugar may have isolated female consumers from the taint of racial otherness, but it did not protect them from the "otherness" that society believed to be in the female body.

A salient example of one woman writer working with a cultural discourse that aligns her body with the body of the slave occurs in *A Poem on the African Slave Trade: Addressed to Her Own Sex*, written by the Quaker Mary Birkett in 1792 to persuade women to join the sugar boycott.[12] The climax of Birkett's poem occurs with a passage deploying anaphora, the repetition of clauses for rhetorical effect. Addressing her female readers, Birkett implores them not to eat sugar, the sinister product of slave labor:

> Shall we who dwell in pleasure, peace, and ease,
> Shall we who but in meekness, mildness please,
> Shall we surrounded by each dear delight,
> To soothe the heart or gratify the sight,
> Say, shall for us the sable sufferers sigh?
> Say, shall for us so many victims die?
> Shall still for us the sable maid bewail?
> Shall still the doating parent's fondness fail? (14)

For Laura Brown anaphora is a central trope in the discourse of mercantile capitalism, used most often by men to deflect, or displace, agency onto women who are subsequently indicted as responsible for imperialism.[13] But here that same trope is used by a woman writer to rally other women for a liberal cause. Has Birkett merely internalized a persistent patriarchal message, or is something more complicated occurring here? The latter seems to be the case, as Birkett's poem evinces a struggle with the contents of a patriarchal ideology. First, note an important side effect of the trope: in its repetition it calls attention to what it would banish. By repeating the phrases "shall we" and "shall for us" Birkett brings insistently to mind the portrait of the female narcissist, even though the answer to her rhetorical questions is obviously a resounding "no!"

Second, Birkett's address to the female consumer answers a rhetorical tradition, seen among other women writers of the period, in which women are indicted for their appetite. Coleman cites an association that often occurs in the literature of the late eighteenth century between "the brutality of slavery and colonization, and the degenerate, depraved, devouring woman." She cites an example from Mrs. Barbauld:

> Lo! where reclined, pale Beauty courts the breeze,
> Diffused on sofas of voluptuous ease;
> With anxious awe her menial train around
> Catch her faint whispers of half-uttered sound;
> See her, in monstrous fellowship unite

At once the Scythian and the Sybarite!
Blending repugnant vices, misallied,
Which frugal nature purposed to divide;
See her, with indolence to fierceness joined,
Of body delicate, inform of mind,
With Languid tones imperious mandates urge;
With arm recumbent wield the household scourge.[14]

Many examples support Coleman's observation. Wollstonecraft, for example, thought women were "rendered weak and luxurious by the relaxing pleasures which wealth procures; but added to this they are made slaves to their persons, and must render them alluring that man may lend them his reason to guide their tottering steps aright."[15] And Adam Smith thought that "luxury in the fair sex, while it inflames perhaps the passion of enjoyment, seems always to weaken, and frequently to destroy altogether, the powers of generation."[16] In Austen's *Mansfield Park* the indolence of Lady Bertram can be directly linked to her pampered status as the wife of a colonialist. In her role as leisured lady of the manor, she has nothing to do: "She was a woman who spent her days in sitting nicely dressed on a sofa, doing some long piece of needlework, of little use and no beauty, thinking more of her pug than her children."[17] The notion that luxury made women into sluggish, barren, and self-absorbed creatures permeates the period.

Thus when a writer like Birkett urges other women to consider the origins of their luxury and ease she refutes the cultural construction of woman as "appetite" and proposes that they refuse to partake of debilitating sensuality. Participating in an ongoing discussion about the nature of the female body, she adopts one particular "subject position"; that is, she presents herself as a particular kind of moral voice, positioning herself to argue for the moral integrity of her gender. However, the presentation of this subject position does preclude other kinds of identification within the same poem, and, indeed, despite her avowed concern for the plight of the slaves, Birkett never totally leaves her other subject position as a white Western European woman. She urges:

Plant there [in Africa] our colonies, and to their soul,
Declare the God who form'd this boundless whole;
Improve their manners—teach them how to live,
To them the useful lore of science gives;

So shall with us their praise and glory rest,
And we in blessing be supremely blest;
For 'tis a duty we surely owe,
We to the Romans were what to us Afric now. (13)

The idea that white civilization will advance African primitivism is at odds with the notion, expressed elsewhere in the poem, that what makes the black slave morally superior is his restraint or self-control, his very ignorance of self-indulgence and laxity. Birkett praises the slave who is "Rear'd in the lap of innocence and ease": "For him no palace rears its costly head, / Contented with an humble turf-built shed / On him no fawning lacqueys proudly wait, / In all the pampered insolence of state" (5). Is the effect of imperial expansion to be an improvement on "primitive" civilization, or does primitive simplicity offer important correctives to the corruptions of imperial decadence? The confusion here may lie in the fact of Birkett's competing subject positions. As a woman who identifies with the black male slave, Birkett projects the theme of her own (culturally constructed) need for distance from luxury. However, as a European colonialist who distances herself from male slaves, Birkett is comfortable making claims for the benefits of her "superior" civilization.

Birkett's identification with the black male slave is seen in other aspects of her poem, namely, her choice of a feminized and domestic hero. As she charts the slave's growth into "ripening manhood" when "freedom was his guest, / And social love glow'd in his faithful breast," she casts him as an affectionate offspring:

He to his parents eye perhaps appears,
The only staff of their declining years;
And he with ceaseless love and anxious care,
Does oft for them the hunted food prepare.

Just as Birkett's readers offer refreshment through the ritual of the tea table, her black slave prepares and offers nourishment. Birkett's narrative is also a story of romantic and familial love, themes familiar to an audience of sentimental fiction: "Perchance soft passion does his bosom move, / And his fond nymph returns his constant love." Or, "perhaps his offspring hail their honour'd sire, / And each to gain the envy'd kiss aspire: / On him a pleasing weight of cares attend, / As father, husband, brother, son, or friend" (6).

Finally, Birkett envisions the moment of his capture; he is, in every way, a tragic victim of sinister forces:

> Haply the hour when their supply he sought
> His soul with ev'ry warm affection fraught
> As over the plain he chac'd his wonted prey,
> And hope deceitful cheer'd the toilsome way;
> When homeward now the lifeless prize he brought,
> And ready greets the cot his rapid thought;
> Him the Christian traders see, his path surround
> In vain his feet pursue their nimble bound;
> He's seized and dragged alone—in vain he cries,
> Starts, stamps the ground, now groans, now weeps, now sighs. (7)

Throughout the poem Birkett's point of view remains with the *male* slave, despite the fact that the life of a female slave would have offered better parallels to her own. Imagined first as someone who is domesticated–as suggested by the detail of his preparing food for his parents—Birkett's slave is then placed within a familial—and nonthreatening—context. Deemphasizing the slave's more "masculine" characteristics in favor of his feminine and nurturing qualities, Birkett portrays him as the victim of others' (ironically the Christian traders') aggression. Her imagery thus represses the hint of potential violence from the slave. As the object of sentimental attention, the male slave is rendered passive. Heroism is depicted not as action, but as mute suffering. In contrast to Birkett's poem, William Cowper's "The Negro's Complaint," first written in 1788, allows the slave a voice, which he uses to reason with the slaving society.[18] Cowper's version of a slave is endowed with sentience and rationality, whereas Birkett's is an object of pity. Whatever Birkett's motive in making the male slave the object of attention, it is clear that his domesticated status makes his situation less threatening to a white audience, which always had to consider the possibility of the slave's violent revolt.

Birkett's poem shows further signs of negotiating a cultural discussion of gender in its use of two central images—blood and cups. Capitalizing on the common abolitionist link between eating sugar and eating the slave's blood or, sometimes, bloodied flesh, Birkett evokes William Fox's famous pamphlet. In *An Address to People of Great Britain on the Propriety of Abstaining from*

West African Sugar and Rum (1791)[19] the Quaker Fox had equated the eating of a pound of sugar with two ounces of human flesh. His other calculations point to the number of lives saved by a family's abstention from sugar: a weekly ration of five pounds not eaten results in the saving of one life; eight families abstaining over nineteen and one-half years save one hundred lives; thirty-eight thousand families refusing to eat sugar stops the trade.

But if Birkett incorporates the theme of sugar consumption as "cannibalism," she also must have been aware that proponents of the sugar trade often referred to sugar as a salubrious "mother's milk." The doctor Benjamin Moseley, in *A Treatise on Sugar with Miscellaneous Medical Observations,* through recourse to a historical "survey" of the cultivation and uses of sugar, argues for the salutary effects of this substance.[20] "Taken in tea, milk, and beer," he writes, sugar "has been found not only sufficient to sustain nature, but has caused lean people to grow fat, and has increased the vigour of their bodies." In addition, he writes,

> In the West Indies, the negro children, from crude vegetable diet, are much inflicted with worms. In crop-time, when the cane are ripe, the children are always sucking them. Give a negro child a piece of sugar cane to suck, and the impoverished milk of his mother is tasteless to him. This salubrious luxury soon changes his appearance. Worms are discharged, his enlarged belly and joints diminish; his emaciated limbs increase, and if sugar were always ripe, he would never be diseased.

In this scenario sugar provides medical benefits that even a mother's milk cannot. The child's preference for the cane is assumed to confirm the fact of sugar's nutritional value. Indeed, Moseley insists upon the restorative powers of sugar: "I have often seen old, scabby wasted negroes crawl from *hot-houses* apparently half-dead, in crop-time; and by sucking canes all day, they soon become strong, fat, and sleaky [*sic*]."[21]

Thus, in pro-slavery literature like Moseley's, colonial power is figured as a "good mother" who sustains and nourishes the very slaves who labor for her. In contrast, a polemic like Fox's creates the image of England as a "bad" mother who cannibalizes her own children. In either case, whether they consume sugar or abstain, real women are enlisted in a national politics. Whether they "nourish" an expanding colonial interest or reject an exploitative colonial policy, their domestic actions mimic in miniature the actions of a state imagined as a maternal body. The image of the cup becomes a flash-point for Birkett precisely because it speaks to the question of whether women inevitably consume or nourish, whether their appetites are enormous and insatiable or manageable and disciplined. If before the cup conveyed the sense that a woman's fluidity was being mastered and ceremoniously presented, it now contains another's bodily fluids. To drink the slave's blood is to fail as a woman and as a mother, but it is also to alter the ritualistic symbolism of the tea table.[22] Birkett writes, "How little think the giddy and the gay / While sipping o'er the sweets of charming tea, / How oft with grief they pierce the manly breast." Thus she makes women's tea drinking the direct cause of the slave's oppression: "How oft their lux'ry robs the wretch of rest / And that to gain the plant we idly waste / Th'*extreme of human mis'ry* they must taste" (2). If the tea table is the appropriate site for the disciplining of the female body, then drinking sweetened tea is a singularly undisciplined act, one with selfish and immoral consequences.

Birkett's choice of an epigraph, misquoted from Sterne's *A Sentimental Journey,* raises further question about the tea drinker's relation to the slave's condition: "Disguise thyself as thou wilt, still, slavery, thou art a bitter cup."[23] The line seems to indicate that the literal cup of tea becomes the metaphoric "cup" of slavery. The drinker of sugary tea forces upon the slave the bitter cup from which he must drink. But is the sweetened cup equally (and ironically) bitter to her? If so, is the fact of slavery itself bitter? Or, feeling herself "enslaved" in some sense as well, does the tea drinker drink the cup of her own bitterness? To whom is the tea bitter? Who, ultimately, is drinking? Is the woman drinking from the bitter cup that results from the slave's labors, or does he drink from the metaphoric cup that she, as "bad mother," forces upon him? These ambiguities are important, for they further suggest a dynamics of projection and identification: either the tea drinker is the slave or she is responsible for the slave.

On the level of its imagery the poem enforces a connection between the tea drinker and the slave in still other ways. Throughout the poem the slave is depicted as having a breast or bosom, the seat of his deep sentiments. No doubt this is a standard image in the rhetoric of the sentimental, from which Birkett borrows freely, and yet Birkett enhances the effect: the slave "bleeds" both literally and metaphorically: "They in their manly breasts conceal their pain; / A silent grief to furious rage succeeds, / And by refinement stung— their whole soul bleeds" (10). But the poet herself bleeds (just as she also drinks from the cup): "A sorrowing sympathy surrounds my heart, / And mild compassion bleeds in every part" (2). This pattern of imagery unites the female abolitionist and the male slave in more ways than one. For if both the woman and the slave bleed, both can also be seen as contaminated. As we know, the slave's blood, brought forth under the dire conditions of his oppression, "contaminates" the tea table.

However, Western culture would have provided Birkett with an even longer tradition of associating female blood, or menstruation, with contamination. Leviticus 15:19–30 stipulates the Mosaic laws designed to counteract women's "impurity." In Judaic tradition female menstruation is a sign of "uncleanness," leading Kristeva to interpret menstrual blood as standing for "the danger issuing from within the identity."[24] In the Middle Ages

> it was believed, in accordance with a tradition already recorded by Pliny, that menstrual blood prevented cereals from sprouting, and soured the must of grapes; that on contact with it, herbs died, trees lost their fruits, iron was attacked by rust and objects of bronze went black; and that dogs who absorbed it contracted rabies. It also had the property of dissolving the glue of bitumen which even iron could not break down.[25]

As late as the seventeenth century these ideas were still being discussed.[26] Though by the eighteenth century most taboos against menstruating women no longer held, the midwife La Motte continued to believe that "some women were dangerous during menstruation and his own maid turned the wine sour."[27] Menstrual blood was linked to women's spiritual condition in still other ways. As Gail Kern Paster explains, "Because menstrual blood was a form of plethora . . . menstruation as a process took on an economy of impurity and waste, so that upper-class women who ate rich, moist foods were thought to flow more heavily than their lower-class counterparts."[28] From this brief history, we learn that Western culture has long associated female bleeding with corruption, contamination, corrosion, decadence, and even power. A woman's menstrual flow provided yet another example of her propensity to "leak": "menstruation comes to resemble the other varieties of female incontinence—sexual, urinary, linguistic—that served as powerful signs of woman's inability to control the workings of her own body," writes Paster.[29]

In the absence of explicit evidence that Mary Birkett held any of these beliefs, we can safely assume that her work exists within a cultural context. While *A Poem on the African Slave Trade* works within a rhetorical tradition that identifies the slave's body as the contaminating presence at the tea table, her poem also alludes to a medical tradition that makes her own body equally suspect. What a woman like Birkett could be said to have learned from the debate about sugar is that her body—site of blood and milk—is not only a source of tropes but also a locus of struggle. In this poem it is women's own insistent desires, located in and arising from the body, that surface. Women, even while they are enjoined to deny themselves sugar, are depicted as existing at the heart of a natural surplus that indulges them at every turn:

> Commerce to you does its choice stores impart,
> With all the gifts of Nature and of Art;
> For you gay Flora animates the scene,
> And spreads with vast parterres the smiling green;
> Her mingled pow'rs and varied charms unite,
> And does each sense—not satiate but delight;
> On you brown Ceres sheds her richest powers,
> Pomona's fruits nectareous—all are yours;
> For you Hygeia, maid of blooming mien,
> With joy rebounding, fills the mirthful scene;
> Can you whose hearts these Heav'n crowned blessings feel,
> Refuse one sacrifice their wounds to heal? (16)

Though the poem moves toward answering its own rhetorical questions with a strong "No," it nonetheless leaves in place the notion of a female subject for whom the world turns. Though the entire poem is predicated upon the notion that women are capable of disciplining their appetites—and that the tea table is precisely the place where that discipline occurs—the poet's own imagery and rhetoric leave a narcissistic female subject in her place.

My point here is not that Birkett "fails"—for I think she succeeds admirably in her liberal purpose of supporting the sugar boycott. Still, in the final analysis her liberal position unfolds within a larger cultural context that makes any discussion of racial politics inseparable from gender politics. I would argue that an urgent unarticulated agenda disturbs the surface of this poem. That unarticulated agenda is the questionable state of the female body: for, as long as the woman who "drinks" is also perceived as the woman who "bleeds," her need for discipline will deflect attention away from other political issues. To abstain from eating sugar is, under the circumstances, a laudable form of behavior, but it fails to address the question of the place of so-called female appetite in the British culture at large.

We return to an image that opened this section: a decorous white woman, demonstrating both her humanitarian concern and her self-discipline, wears close to her bosom the image of a supplicating negro slave. But the Wedgwood cameo fixes the male sufferer in a mute, frozen pose. The figure never speaks; his narrative is miniaturized and reduced to a painful tableau. Possibilities for heroic action are forestalled, declarations of personhood, indictments of imperial racism never made. And if the male slave never tells his story, the female slave is still farther off on the horizon. Her body, whether it labors under slavery or rises up in revolt, remains unrepresented.[30] We would have to go far beyond the parameters of the tea table to hear her story.

China

In *The Rape of the Lock* Belinda occupies two places within an economy of exchange. She is both, as critics have often indicated, an item to be traded and a consumer of commodities. Within the poem one image—that of fine china or porcelain—best conveys her dual status. On the one hand, Belinda is like a precious piece of china, ready to be broken at any moment. In canto 2 dire events are foreshadowed by Ariel, who likens Belinda's virginity to a piece of china: "Whether the Nymph shall break *Diana's* Law, / Or some frail *China* Jar receive a Flaw." After Belinda's lock—symbolizing her maidenhead—has been cut, the affinity between virginity and china is evoked once more: "Not louder Shrieks to pitying Heav'n are cast, / When Husbands or when Lap-dogs breathe their last, / Or when rich *China* Vessels, fal'n from high, / In glittring Dust and painted Fragments lie."[1]

On the other hand, the poem asserts Belinda's keen appreciation for the very commodity that acts as a metaphor for her condition. In canto 3 her guests enjoy coffee: "From silver Spouts the grateful Liquors glide, / While *China's* Earth receives the smoking Tyde. / At once they gratify their Scent and Taste, / And frequent Cups prolong the rich Repast" (lines 109–112). Belinda's status as a consumer of imported luxuries has already been discussed, but it is also clear that her taste extends to expensive porcelain.[2]

Thus Belinda's situation as marketable commodity is matched by her status as participant *in* the marketplace. If the presence of china in the poem encapsulates Belinda's condition (as Cleanth Brooks has suggested), it also signals a range of qualities that, to this day, stereotypically attend the woman shopper, namely, an obsession with what is expensive and beautiful, a taste for what is sensual or luxurious, a longing to possess extraordinary articles of value.[3]

As in *The Rape of the Lock*, throughout a variety of eighteenth-century texts fine china or porcelain denotes women and their weaknesses. Often the image of china functions as a marker for female superficiality or for a potential female depravity located in an inordinate attraction to "things." Ironically, while the rituals of the tea table dictated a female preoccupation with the appearances of things—gestures carefully choreographed, tea equipage displayed just so—that same preoccupation could be cited as a dangerous indication of a woman without "depth." Any item could have been deployed to denote the feminine, but historical coincidence made china an appropriate marker in the effort to define "woman." Located at the very center of her prescribed domain, china made it possible for people to talk about women and their qualities in a particular way.

Formalist analysis, represented by the work of Brooks or Aubrey Williams, has long given us access to this trope. A New Historical reconsideration of china as a trope for woman can take us further, however. Such an approach insists that literary representation refers us not to a fixed historical "reality" but to ideological process: in this case, what we discern when we interpret literary texts is not the "the history of women and their things" but rather a history of the *representation* of women and their things. Exemplifying this more recent approach is the work of Laura Brown. In *The Ends of Empire: Women and Ideology in Early Eighteenth-Century England* Brown demonstrates how eighteenth-century discourse attributes "mercantile capitalism itself, with all of its attractions, as well as its ambiguous consequences" to women, "whose marginality allows them to serve, in the writings of celebrants and satirists alike, as a perfect proxy or scapegoat."[4] Brown deploys the trope of dressing in particular to demonstrate how "female adornment becomes the main emblem of commodity fetishism."[5]

Privileging china, rather than dressing, as a defining trope for femininity introduces a separate set of themes. First, china deflects the issue of a female essentialism that inevitably underlies the dressing metaphor. Whereas underneath the adorned female figure one might imagine discovering "some underlying, essential, and untransmutable female nature,"[6] china is either surface (a plate) or empty, hollow space (a cup or bowl). The very utility of china as a trope for femininity seems to have stemmed from its property as surface. China offered a blank textual surface upon which culture could write its notions of gender. At the same time, however, china inevitably reminds us of the "fictile" process through which gender is constructed. As a substance, porcelain carries no significance until it has been shaped or molded, painted and fired, affixed with a price. So too women (and men) in the eighteenth century were subjected to a shaping process, which also ascribed to them their value. In turning from material history to literary texts portraying women and china, we encounter, then, fictions about a "fictional" process—literally, representations of a how, in the presence of a very precise image, a culture came to shape and mold its constructions of gender.

Considering a representative sample of texts from the late seventeenth century to the early nineteenth century, we see how the female as an *object* of male desire became, over the course of the long eighteenth century, the female as desiring *subject*. This process has been identified before, in the work of Nancy Armstrong, Ruth Perry, Felicity Nussbaum, and others, but I will argue that tracing the expression of that desire through the image of china helps us to locate a particularly modern definition of the domestic woman several decades before its putative origins during the latter decades of the eighteenth century. The first part of this section explores the historical conditions that generated china as an appropriate trope for the feminine: what is the material history of china, and what accounted for its metaphoric potential? In the second part the focus shifts to a discussion of three representative texts that deploy the image of china—"Ardelia's Answer to Ephelia" by Anne Finch, *Camilla* by Frances Burney, and *Marriage* by Susan Ferrier. Though poised at opposite ends of the long eighteenth century, these texts consistently align a particularly superficial construction of femininity with an urban mercantile setting. Reading these texts against the material history of china can help us to see how society projected its own ambivalence about consumer culture onto women.

We begin with a simple observation: the "china fever" that swept eighteenth-century England was by no means particular to women or even to a special class of people.[7] Over the course of the eighteenth century china became a commodity of unprecedented popularity for nearly everyone in England. Working out of the Orphan's Court Inventories, Lorna Weatherill writes that "china. . . . changed from being unknown in 1675 to being a normal part of household equipment by 1715."[8] Sometimes synonymous with the word *porcelain*, china appealed to the upper and lower classes alike.[9] While the upper classes followed the craze for expensive and elegant porcelain, often in the form of chinoiserie, the other classes saw a "revolution" in tableware.[10] Thus the history of china in eighteenth-century England unfolds in two ways—as an aesthetic object and as an item for everyday use.

The fashion of collecting fine china or porcelain as aesthetic object has been documented by historians like J. H. Plumb. He writes that in 1700 one ship alone unloaded 146,748 pieces of porcelain: "By 1750 all Europe was in the grip of china-fever. No mania for material objects had ever been so widespread, so general to the rich of all nations."[11] Yet this "china fever" had its roots in the seventeenth-century; indeed references to the selling of china in England occur as early as 1609.[12] English travelers on the continent had seen porcelain "well before the Restoration," writes one historian. The Dutch used porcelain daily by 1614, and, under the influence of an exiled Huguenot, William's wife Mary had collected porcelain.[13]

In 1675 the playwright William Wycherley capitalized on the late seventeenth-century infatuation with china to comic effect. In a well-known scene from *The Country Wife* china is deployed as a metaphor for illicit behavior,

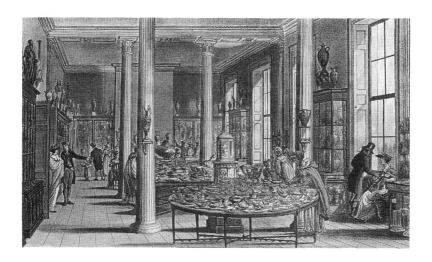

"Wedgwood and Byerley" from *Ackermann's Repository of Arts. Courtesy of the Yale Center for British Art, Paul Mellon Collection*

specifically for adulterous sex with the lascivious Mr. Horner. Several decades before china made its way into British households on a wide scale, Wycherley associates china with a female "appetite." For him, as for Joseph Addison after him, china is useful in a polemic about the boundaries of female subjectivity. China is less the marker for woman's status as *object*—as china tropes the male body here—and more the indicator of an ideological struggle to shape woman's situation as a desiring *subject* within a particular domestic economy.

When Lady Fidget claims she has been "toiling and moiling for the prettiest piece of china, my dear," the audience recognizes all too well the real object of her desire. Horner plays into her double entendre with his retort, "Nay, she has been too hard for me, do what I could," implying that he cannot satisfy her sexual appetite. Mrs. Squeamish then demands, "O Lord, I'll have some china too. Good Mr. Horner, don't think to give other people china, and me none; come in with me too." To which he responds, "Upon my honor, I have none left now."[14] They continue in this vein, the playwright exploiting the metaphoric potential of "china" in relation to a randy sexuality.

Indeed, what makes the scene work especially well is the connection between china as a precious, coveted commodity and Horner's irrepressible phallicism. Like expensive china, Horner's body is sought after by the ladies. The "hardness" of the china makes it an appropriate phallic image. That Horner feels himself beleaguered by the voracious Lady Fidget and Mrs. Squeamish is also part of the scene's comic effect. Wycherley's use of china as a metaphor for the male body establishes both the desirable qualities of the commodity and a distinctly *female* demand for it.

In a similar vein, in the *Spectator* the image of china is key to a discussion about controlling female desire to acquire and collect. Here the issue is the husband's need to keep control over household resources. In "The Lover," number 10, the wives' desire to possess china prompts them to circumvent their husband's economic control, as they trade their old clothes for the coveted "brittle ware." Addison's narrator writes of an "old petticoat metamorphosed into a punch-bowl, and a pair of breeches into a teapot." One man, writes Addison, "calls his great room, that is nobly furnished with china, his wife's wardrobe.

> "In yonder corner, (says he), are above twenty suits of clothes, and on
> that scrutoire above a hundred yards of furbelowed silk. You cannot

imagine how many night-gowns went into the raising of that pyramid. The worst of it is, (says he), that a suit of clothes is not suffered to last half its time, that it may be more vendible; so that in reality, this is but a more dextrous way of picking the husband's pocket, who is often purchasing a great vase of china, when he fancies he is buying a fine head, or a silk gown for his wife."[15]

In this way china is at the center of a struggle over familial resources. That women have no resources of their own with which to buy their prized china is not the point. Rather, the narrator sympathizes with the husband who feels himself cheated by his wife's actions. While the husband expects to see his profits displayed in his wife's gown or on her head, she thwarts his expectations. The female subject whose behavior Addison laments is a subversive agent who displaces the public eye from her own body—the "proper" site for the spectacular register of familial wealth—to her porcelain collection instead.

Arguments like Addison's are all the more remarkable in light of a historical record that gives little credence to the notion that female consumers had any special inclination to collect china; here we can invoke material history as evidence of a cultural fiction at work. Rather, women may have been associated with china because the rituals of their daily life made its presence an asset. On a second level, then, the history of china is also the story of a revolution in domestic tableware; this history addresses the actual use, rather than collection, of china. According to Carole Shammas, while the use of brass, pewter, and wooden products declined in the early decades of the eighteenth century, new tableware gained acceptance: "This shift involved the replacement of quite sturdy durables with more decorative but more disposable crockery and glass." Because women were associated with the domestic sphere, one might expect to find female possession of such crockery, and Shammas finds that "female inventoried deceased were more likely to have owned such things as teacups, tea kettles, and so forth, even if variables such as wealth held constant."[16] However, Lorna Weatherill, in a more exhaustive analysis of inventory tables from middle-ranking tradesmen and farmers, finds "very little aggregate difference" between men and women in ownership patterns of china. She concludes, "It may be that the assumption that women were interested in china and hot drinks as early as [1740] is mistaken. Men were certainly interested in collecting china and formed the clientele of coffee houses."[17] Thus it may well be the case that men *collected* china, while women actually *used* it on a wider scale.

Like other imported commodities—silk, tea, and cotton—china drew the female consumer into a national debate about the debilitating effects of a home economy indebted to foreign trade. As Louis Landa writes, mercantilistic economic thought of the period often assumed that "the importation of luxuries [was] not economically desirable, the logic being that imported luxuries have an adverse effect on the balance of trade."[18] Because women were stereotypically identified as the principle consumers of such imported products, they most often bore the brunt of an antimercantilist polemic.

Yet china also differs from other imported commodities because of its distinctive history. The very etymology of the word *china* suggests how the exotic, the domestic, and the history of empire became embedded in one another. In pausing to trace this history, we not only provide another account of what has been called Orientalism but we also perceive the important function of the domestic in the production of Orientalist discourse. As we will see, women play an central role in the creation of that discourse. According to the OED, *China* is not a native Chinese name: used to designate the country in Asia, the word *China* is found in Sanskrit about the Christian era. Through synecdoche, *china* comes to mean the commodity that comes from China. The OED stipulates that a Persian word for Chinese porcelain, China-ware, or china, diffused as *chini,* moved through India and eventually made its way to seventeenth-century England.[19] In other words, the history of the word *china* encapsulates the ancient trading routes, as well as their subsequent opening to the West. It carries within it a history of trade and commerce. That *china* is simultaneously known as *porcelain* and *china* testifies to the dual trading histories of England and Portugal. The first to expand into the East, the Portuguese gave china the name it was to assume on the continent—porcelain. But British traders, moving into India after the marriage of the Portuguese Catherine of Braganza to Charles II, would have had access to either name.[20]

Over the course of the eighteenth century the word *china* gradually becomes a dead metaphor, as it denotes less and less a product coming exclusively from the Far East. With the discovery of beds of kaolin (an ingredient key to the making of true porcelain, one that vitrifies at a higher temperature than other clays) in Cornwall in 1754, the British were at last able to make a product of reasonable semblance to the imported ware.[21] While Wedgwood established highly effective means for advertising and promoting an indigenous pottery, factories in China began producing chinaware to British specifications.[22] Gradually, what was unusual and distinct about china—both its material and its design—was adapted to and mastered by Western taste.

With the late eighteenth-century success of the East India Trading Company, the country China became most accessible to the Western gaze just at the moment when the product china gained its widest popularity at home. However, through the discourses of Orientalism the end result of direct contact with Eastern cultures was not a more accurate "knowledge" of Chinese civilizations but an appropriation of its cultural heritage.[23] China came to figure imagistically in the British popular imagination as an exotic, luxurious landscape. Its people were transformed (in the words of Charles Lamb) into "those little, lawless, azure-tinctured grotesques, that under the notion of men and women float about, uncircumscribed by any element, in that world before perspective, the china tea-cup."[24] Thus, the history of porcelain in England reveals the material base of Orientalism: British mastery of a specific material—kaolin—facilitated British mastery of Orientalist images.

A brief history of blue willow ware suggests how the Western popular imagination transformed fanciful images of a foreign country into familiar scenes for domestic consumption. Though the still-popular pattern is in fact a nineteenth-century creation, the prototype for this pattern occurs as early as 1785.[25] In their late eighteenth-century variations, chinese-styled willow pattern designs represent English interpretations of Chinese landscapes. For example, the Willow-Nankin pattern, produced in the factories at Caughley, shows a bucolic island and exotic buildings, with (in the words of one connoisseur) two dovelike birds "performing a remarkable U-turn!"[26] Other factories turned out the willow pattern for export as well as for the domestic market: the Spode factory ultimately produced fourteen versions. One historian writes, "The porcelain trade turned a full circle in 1823 when Spode supplied the East India Company in Canton with 1,300 pieces of service [in the willow pattern] for the sum of 400 pounds."[27] However, this kind of exchange can scarcely be said to have advanced any true cultural understanding. To the contrary, willow ware circulated a peculiarly British version of Chinese lore: with "no Chinese prototype either in decoration or legend," the pattern has been designated "a purely Western invention."[28] Yet this "purely Western invention" came, for many, to represent the quintessential experience of the Orient.

Once it was brought to the tea table, a china pattern like that of the Willow-Nankin became the domain of women: they were to oversee the domestication of the foreign and the exotic. As the scented tea poured from the latest teapot, the woman herself was poised at the place where the East would yield to the West; Orientalism was brought home in feminine hands. Thus fine china at the tea table, especially if it was domestically produced, added an underlying symbolism to the ritual: on a national level it evoked the "glories" of mercantile expansion, demonstrating how the foreign had been brought home, transformed, possessed.[29] On a familial level it testified to the status of a particular family who participated in that same mercantile expansion. The pleasing surfaces of plates and cups reflected the wealth and taste of those who possessed them.

The woman herself, well-disciplined in the delicate art of the tea table, could also be on display. Louis Landa points out the metaphoric potential of china, the qualities that made it a trope for the teleology of the female condition itself: "made of the dust and clay of earth," china vessels suggest "loss of perfection, beauty and virginity. . . . "There is the hint of mortality inherent in all the imagery which likens women to something so frangible as fine glass or China."[30] A woman's close proximity to china thus enabled a semiotic process that allowed her to be "read" as a particular kind of surface: like the china she holds in her lovely hands, the woman at the tea table is flawless and delicate. She is aesthetically perfect, yet also sometimes hollow and empty, waiting to be filled. Her perfect surface makes her appear superior, yet, after all, she is ultimately made of clay; she is of this world, merely mortal. Also, like the frangible item she holds in her hands, she can be "molded" into shape, made to assume the pose or attitude that best expresses her family's status.

Against this brief material history, literary examples deploying the image of the female china lover take on an additional significance. Details that might have appeared textually "innocent" reverberate with new meaning. Here an early eighteenth-century example, from the poetry of Anne Finch, is followed by two late eighteenth-century examples. Though social and political differences separate the three authors, all three participate, to one degree or another, in an ongoing process of constructing female subjectivity. For all three the definition of female agency depends on a configuration of materialism. For all three, as well, a woman's love of china, an undue fixation with the surface of things, marks her as a negative female subject, as a woman of "no depth." Thus, although scholars of the eighteenth-century have suggested that the preoccupation with a woman's depth was a phenomenon of the late eighteenth century, these three examples suggest that the process of observing depth as a sign of female interiority may have begun earlier. By the end of the century the female china lover was a familiar type in a domestic discourse promoting the selfless female subject. Throughout the long eighteenth century the woman who loved china was associated with the urban sphere—with its intense pressures to consume competitively— while the nonmaterialistic woman preferred, like the narrator of Anne Finch's "Ardelia's Answer to Ephelia," to live "from all distraction free" in the peaceful shade of the country.

Critics have read Finch's satire as an answer to Rochester's "Letter from Artemis in the Town to Chloe in the Country."[31] In the poem the "country nymph," Ardelia, writes to a country friend to tell of the vain, dissipated, and materialistic life of a "court nymph," Almeria. Under the satiric eye of the poem's "country" narrator, Almeria commodifies herself for the male gaze. As she poses for her male admirers, the glass of her coach windows (still a luxury in the late seventeenth century) frames her attractions, giving her the allure of an item in a shop window:

> Whilest the gay thing, light as her feathered dress,
> Flies round the coach, and does each cushion press,
> Through every glass her several graces shows,
> This does her face, and that, her shape expose,
> To envying beauties and admiring *beaux*.

Almeria is depicted as oblivious to the effects of her own commodification. Indeed, at the heart of the satire lies the notion that, by participating in the competitive display of materialistic goods, she becomes complicitous in selling herself cheaply.

The poem further allows Almeria to indict herself. While Ardelia slips into a church to pray, Almeria spills her woes to the nearest fop, complaining most bitterly about her friend's inability to appreciate the material texture of her city life. She especially laments how her country acquaintance

Then, drinks the fragrant tea contented up,
Without a compliment upon the cup,
Though to the ships for the first choice I steered,
Through such a storm, as the stout bargemen feared;
Lest that a praise, which I have long engrossed,
Of the best china equipage, be lost.
Of fashions now and colors I discoursed,
Detected shops that would expose the worst,
What silks, what lace, what ribbons she must have,
And by my own, an ample pattern gave;
To which, she cold and unconcerned replied,
Ideal with one that all these does provide,
Having of other cares, enough beside;
And in a cheap or an ill chosen gown
Can value blood that's nobler than my own,
And therefore hope, myself not to be weighed
By gold or silver on my garments laid;
Or that my wit or judgment should be read
In an uncommon color on my head.[32]

Here we have a virtual catalogue of the commodities thought especially attractive to city women—not only tea and china but other items of fashion also denoting the materialistic "woman of surface." Like the wife in Addison's "The Lover," Almeria is obsessed with her china, going to any length to obtain it. The mock heroics of her attempt—storms braved and so on—only render her passion more absurd. Finch juxtaposes Almeria's superficiality to Ardelia's spirituality, in particular, to her deep sense of internal worth. Moreover, as the poem progresses, Almeria's lack of depth is matched by her other negative qualities—her cattiness, her willingness to betray a female friend, her inability to recognize true wit because it does not praise her, her sycophantic pursuit of the rich and famous. Last of all, Almeria attacks the very idea of the female poet.

Now it might be possible to argue, as one critic has, that Finch's poem offers "ethical touchstones" in response to Rochester's misogynist invective.[33] In offering us Ardelia as a "woman of depth," does not Finch refute age-old stereotypes and put forth a positive ideal? Is not Finch's point to demonstrate how women need not act out the part that male poets have written for them? However, though this approach defends the poem against the charge that it is antifeminist, it does not give sufficient weight to the manner in which Finch has structured her polemic.[34]

Few readers seem to notice, for example, that Almeria's tirade against Ardelia's resistance to materialism (lines 63–98) would have to be delivered in Ardelia's own voice: if Almeria's speech were delivered while Ardelia is *in church* (lines 42–43), the tirade could only be *imagined* by Ardelia, who would not be there to hear it. The clumsiness of this device attests less to Finch's "lack of skill" as a poet and more to her polemical intentions. Arguably, Almeria is never given the opportunity to "speak," even though, later in the poem, we receive her words "verbatim." That is, Almeria never becomes more than a satiric type, a "court nymph" whose position is determined as much by literary tradition as by any "real" experience. In her position as a "woman of surface" she serves a polemical purpose: to discredit all that is associated with the urban scene, as well as the material and political life it engendered. Even if we acknowledge that both Almeria and Ardelia are equally constructed versions of a female subjectivity, it is perfectly obvious that they are not weighted equally.[35]

From "Ardelia's Answer to Ephelia" we learn that the city is a place where, through the avid appreciation of commodities like china, women learn to "sell" themselves cheaply. However, knowledge of the material history of china, especially of its actual audience, denaturalizes this idea: if historical evidence reveals that appreciation for china was not restricted to one geographical location, if historians remind us that men also avidly appreciated china, the intentions of this scene become more accessible. Behind this satire directed at urban life is an ideological attack on the mercantile class and a nascent consumer culture. Yet even a most cursory reading of Finch's biography would give the modern reader a sense of the author's motivation for this attack. Having been exiled to Eastwell Park, Kent, since 1690, Finch and her husband never regained the political prestige they had enjoyed during the reign of the Stuarts. Finch would have had everything to gain in promoting her own necessary rural employment. As the place of the opposition, the urban scene, not surprisingly, represents the values Finch's narrator "chooses" to reject. Thus, what initially appears as a "feminist" answer to a misogynist poetic tradition gradually emerges as a more complicated political statement. Indeed, the resistance of a poem like this to *either* label— antifeminist or feminist is instructive, for such resistance suggests the necessity of placing the term *feminist* within a historically specific social and political context.

As the century draws to a close, the association of china and superficiality persists, gathering momentum in a discourse designed to produce "self-regulating" female subjects, ready to participate in a domestic economy. In a late-century example, Frances Burney in *Camilla* (1796) uses the character of Indiana (whose very name aligns her with expensive and exotic tastes) to represent a truly superficial woman. She literally cannot go beyond the surface of things. In a key scene she fixates on the material effects of a poor family—their missing china in particular—while the morally superior Camilla devotes herself to a baby.

> Dear! Crockery ware! How ugly!—Lord, what little mean chairs!—
> Is that your best gown, good woman?—Dear, what an ugly pattern!—
> Well, I would not wear such a thing to save my life!—Have you got
> nothing better than this for a floor-cloth?—Only look at those cur-
> tains! Did you ever see such frights?—Lord! do you eat off those plat-
> ters! I am sure I could sooner die! I should not mind starving half as
> much![36]

While Indiana is scarcely one of Burney's most subtle characters, she serves an important ideological purpose in the novel. She is foil to Camilla, a character so thoroughly portrayed as a woman of depth that she is given no physical description in the novel. Camilla seems to have no surface except that which is constantly given to her through the male gaze. Here Burney establishes the contrast between two modes of female subjectivity, deploying household items as meaningful images. As a type Indiana stands in for an older, aristocratic tradition, in which the female body itself was put on display as a sign of aristocratic power. Her preoccupation with the cottagers' material effects—their tableware in particular—suggests she cannot move beyond a world where display is all. Camilla, in contrast, has little interest in superficial display and is much more concerned with an interiorized sense of self.[37]

That Indiana is so exaggerated a character suggests Burney's polemical intentions; the text works to position the reader's sympathies entirely with Camilla. Indeed, Indiana's addiction to materialism is depicted as so severe that it threatens her body: she claims she would rather starve than eat off inferior tableware. Her self-centered anorexic display is contrasted with the far healthier charity of Camilla, who is reluctant to give up the baby she has been "nursing." (Indeed, since the word *nursing* continued to carry the double sense of "tending to" and "suckling," Camilla's nursing forecasts her abilities as a mother.) Yet the price Camilla pays for being the woman of depth is an intense preoccupation with the way in which she is viewed through the male gaze. This preoccupation will lead, after several volumes of misperceptions and misunderstandings, to her "breakdown," a near-death experience in which Camilla confronts her own final judgment. Thus, though the woman of surface bears the brunt of this novel's satire, the woman of depth endures a more arduous trial.[38]

The most spectacular representation of a female china lover occurs in Susan Ferrier's *Marriage* (1818). In Ferrier's hands the female appreciation of china accumulates all its meanings: Lady Juliana becomes the apotheosis of all that the new domestic woman must not be, as one scene especially demonstrates. While she considers a range of bibelots brought into her London drawing room by a china merchant, her husband and his benefactor look on. The scene is especially ironic, since her husband is poised on the edge of financial ruin; the benefactor is paying a courtesy call to the family before offering them financial assistance. Lady Juliana, "educated for the sole purpose of forming a brilliant establishment," and by now hopelessly spoiled, is accustomed to buying whatever strikes her fancy. One item especially catches her fancy. The merchant presents it:

> "Please to observe this choice piece—it represents a Chinese cripple, squat on the ground, with his legs crossed. Your ladyship may observe the head and chin advanced forward, as in the act of begging. The tea pours from the open mouth; and, till your ladyship tries, you can have no idea of the elegant effect it produces."
>
> "That is really droll," said Lady Juliana, with a laugh of delight; "and I must have the dear, sick beggar, he is so deliciously hideous."[39]

Also presented for her consideration is (in the words of the salesman) "an amazing delicate article, in the way of a jewel: a frog of Turkish agate for burning pastiles in." This, she is told, is especially valuable "for it was the favourite toy of one of the widowed sultanas, till she grew devout and gave up perfumes" (139). The frog is followed by a set of jars, teapots, mandarins, sea monsters, and pug dogs. But the crowning piece is a massive China teapot, which "appeared to be a serpent coiled in a regular fold round the body of a tiger placed on end." Lady Juliana is assured that "such a specimen not one half the size has ever been imported to Europe . . . it was secretly procured from one of the temples, where, gigantic as it may seem, and uncouth for the purpose, it was the idol's principle tea-pot!" (140).

The objects Ferrier describes in this scene are both the reminders of a particularly idiosyncratic kind of material culture and potent symbols. To begin, these are especially grotesque images of china—not just translucent dinner plates or dainty teacups but distorted bits of chinoiserie. The reader can scarcely miss the implications of an avid appreciation for items such as these, and there is no way to redeem this particular kind of consumption. The exaggerated surfaces of these items signal a genuine perversion of taste. Lady Juliana's enthusiasm for these items associates her with Oriental aestheticism: she now appreciates the very trinkets that tired the sultana. Thus the passage simultaneously stereotypes Oriental aesthetics as decadent and renders Lady Juliana's tastes even more perverse. Moreover, she marvels at the "uncouth" teapot of a pagan idol. The teapot in the shape of the Chinese beggar represents the most morally corrupt appropriation of Chinese culture for the sole purpose of being fashionable. That the Chinese man is a *beggar* alerts us to her lack of humanity: to her it is "deliciously hideous." Her consumption is precisely a form of eating—a parasitism in which she lives off the misery of others. The tea that pours from his mouth, the very substance of the Chinese man's country, quenches her thirst without her conscience ever interceding.

Lady Juliana's failure to recognize the suffering represented—and, conversely, her ability to see the act of begging as something "droll"—ties directly to another major theme of the novel: her failed "maternal instincts," her inability to sacrifice anything of herself in order to serve the needs of another. Throughout the novel Ferrier juxtaposes Lady Juliana's uncontrollable "urge to shop" with her failure to feel anything at all for her children. Her spending of money is connected to her dissipation of resources better directed toward her maternal and domestic duties. Time, energy, and attention paid to the pursuit of her own material pleasures are time, energy, and attention that cannot be put into domestic duty. Thus it is highly significant that Lady Juliana refuses to breast-feed her twin daughters, for, in the idiom of the book, her milk is a wasted family resource. What Lady Juliana "wastes" on herself she cannot afford to spend on anyone else, and the hapless Chinese beggar is just another victim of a failed humanity so deep that it is impervious even to what should be (so the novel tells us) the most profound of human sentiments—the love of a mother for her children. In addition, Lady Juliana's failure to nurture becomes a "national" failure when she fails to rear what ought to her country's greatest resource—its children.

This is a complicated scene whose ideological purpose runs in two directions. On the one hand, a formal reading suggests it contains what could be called a critique of imperial excesses: Lady Juliana is the satiric portrait of a class long accustomed to gratifying its own taste, regardless of the price those tastes exact in an international market. Without signaling any explicit sympathy for those who suffer under imperial expansion, Ferrier nonetheless aligns herself with those, like the Chinese beggar, who are callously disregarded by Western consumers. On the other hand, placing this passage in its historical context, we find that this satiric critique is enabled through the scapegoating of a *female* character.[40] Lady Juliana (and implicitly other women of her type) bears the burden for morally bankrupt imperial expansion. Ferrier creates Lady Juliana's inveterate spending as the moral catastrophe at the heart of the novel. Lady Juliana becomes the "negative center" against which all the positive characters in the book—including her own daughter Mary—develop. Her perfidy is necessary to give shape and meaning to the moral acts of the "good" characters who ultimately triumph, finding happiness where none was available to Lady Juliana.

As we have seen through a survey of the image of china, mercantile capitalism had indulged, even sanctioned, a "feminine" appreciation of imported commodities like china when such an appreciation promoted mercantile interests. Properly domesticated at the tea table, the female china lover promoted her husband's status and furthered the goals of imperial expansion. But Lady Juliana is not properly domesticated; her desires have not been reigned in, and she trespasses the boundaries of the tea table. Still, her function as scapegoat is clear: in locating the unrestrained desire to consume in Lady Juliana and her hideous objects, Ferrier effectively suggests that such desire exists nowhere else.

Viewed in a historical context, then, Lady Juliana emerges as a political type; she takes her place in a long line of female china lovers whose ideological purpose is to signal an ongoing debate about the role of women in the economy: avid consumers, conspicuous and necessary displayers of mercantile riches, or conservative managers of a familial economy? Ferrier deploys chinoiserie rather than the more utilitarian tableware to weigh the argument on the side of a new domestic conservatism. Lavish display is powerfully discredited as an outmoded form of corrupt aristocratic privilege; Lady Juliana's daughter Mary will more modestly manage her family's accounts.

Throughout the long eighteenth century, china is much more than a metaphor for the female condition. It is also a crucial reminder that femininity is an ongoing historical construction, one subject to changing economic interests and pressures. The transformation of the female as *object* to the female as *subject* involves as well the historical construction of *woman as consumer*: in an age when a woman's "duty" increasingly involved her management of household resources, female patterns of consumption became a statement about a woman's identity. In displaying her family's wealth appropriately—neither withholding the evidence of mercantile enterprise, nor wantonly pursuing consumption as a form of self-gratification—a woman proved her self-worth. During an age of imperial expansion a woman's agency to consume became both her political imperative and the potential cause of her personal demise. We have seen how the female china lover takes the fall for what should have been identified as social excess.

Recent work done in cultural studies reminds us that the relationship between people and the goods they consume defies easy analysis. As Mary Douglas and Baron Isherwood write, "Goods . . . are the visible part of culture. They are arranged in vistas and hierarchies that can give play to the full range of discrimination of which the human mind is capable. The vistas are not fixed; nor are they randomly arranged in a kaleidoscope. Ultimately, their structures are anchored to human purposes."[41] What they say has direct relevance to the eighteenth century and to the case of china in particular. The properties of porcelain allow us to meditate on yet another fictile process, namely, the process by which a society comes to terms with the meaning of commodity culture. For, also like clay, commodity culture has no intrinsic significance until it has been subjected to interpretation. Thus, throughout the eighteenth century, china allows for social exploration of *what consumption means*. Women, ever present in relation to the display of china, are constructed to carry the weight for cultural ambivalence about the meaning of consumption. The delicate items they hold in their hands suggest not only how frangible is their own condition but also how plastic is the emerging consumer culture in which they find themselves.

In conclusion, the history of the tea table in eighteenth-century England unfolds on two levels. On the first, it is a history of specific objects that become commonplace in British households: tea, sugar, and china. But, on a second level, it is also a history of how a culture generated and then sought to maintain one particular definition of female subjectivity based on an essentialized understanding of the female body. What was at stake, then, in the history of women and the tea table was not just the implementation of certain forms of behavior, or the control of female movement, but also the attempt to define and regulate female desire within certain boundaries. The discourse of the tea table configures, then seeks to confine, female desire as a powerful yet illicit force to be used according to woman's place in society. However, as suggested by the two fictional passages that launched this discussion, the discourse of the tea table is also continually fraught with tension and ambiguity, with a sense of mystery and potential disruption. As Irigaray reminds us, "Fluid—like that other inside/outside of philosophical discourse—is by nature, unstable."[42] Thus a cultural construction of femininity that depended upon tropes of fluidity, which, indeed, made liquids themselves the sign of femininity, was perpetually subject to its own subversion. The woman at the tea table might be a daughter or a witch, a properly socialized "lady" or a subversive, working-class harridan. She might be a subject onto whom one could displace great erotic longings or she might be a figure from whom one would turn with revulsion and horror. What she could never be was an independent agent, actively creating her own definition of subjectivity; for that process of crystallizing an identity within what Irigarary calls the "mechanics" of fluids eluded her.

Shopping

Introduction: Commodities

On August 4, 1774, touring the ruins of Ruthlan Castle in North Wales, Dr. Johnson described the remnants of a depraved and barren domesticity, "Only one tower had a chimney, so that here was [no] commodity in living. It was only a place of strength."[1] Here *commodity* carries its obsolete meaning: "as a quality or condition of things, in relation to the needs of men, etc.: the quality of being 'commodious': conveniency, suitability, fitting utility, commodiousness." That sense of the word *commodity*—as a quality in relation to human need—coexisted during the eighteenth century with another; concurrently, *commodity* was also "a thing of use or advantage to mankind; esp. in *pl.* useful products, material advantages, elements of wealth." The two senses of the word complemented each other, since a thing of no use could not be a commodity, it literally could not be "commodious."[2]

Johnson's quote is an apt point of departure for a feminist analysis of women and commodities, since it implicitly establishes a series of connections relevant to the history of women: "Only one tower had a chimney, so that there was [no] commodity in living." Without the presence of chimneys, making possible all the pleasures of the hearth, a castle, whatever its riches, could have no commodity. Such a place would be devoid of cheer, lacking not only the warmth and conveniences of "home" but also, presumably, the very domestic pleasures that arise when the family gathers there. Such a castle might well be "a place of strength," but it would never be a place of comfort.

Women, of course, have a special relation to that same scene. Often depicted in relation to a domesticated fire—fireplace or hearth—women have been long associated with the civilizing processes made possible by the development of indoor space. Either as preparers of food or providers of a range of domestic pleasures, women have historically been an important element in "commodity." They have often existed in relation to the needs of men, their very presence depending upon being useful, convenient, or commodious. Thus it is worth remarking that the trope woman as commodity is only truly meaningful when the historical evolution of *commodity* is observed. Women have been historically situated in relation to changing definitions of what is convenient, suitable, useful, or commodious, and woman's value as commodity has evolved in response to these changing definitions, as well as upon her social and racial position.[3]

My question, then, concerns the emerging definition of the female subject in what can rightly be called "the age of the commodity," as the eighteenth century saw both an important shift in the concept of the commodity and in new consumer activities designed to circulate commodities, chief among them the pastime known as shopping.[4] What light does the history of commodity shed upon woman's own status as commodity in an emerging consumer society? In this first section I will propose that a modern understanding of "woman" depended very much on the gradual evolution of the notion of commodity. Just as the modern sense of *commodity* depended upon a cultural shift in concepts of usefulness and luxury, so too did the modern definition of female subjectivity depend upon changes in the concepts of woman's use and superfluity. Before elaborating on this shift, I turn in the second section, "Shops and Shoppers," to the specific social practices that initially linked women to the world of goods. As we will see, if shopping first emerged as an indoor process, it also entailed the proliferation of interiorized psychological strategies for selling and buying. From the beginning these strategies were understood as gendered activities. The last section, "Pornography," returns to women as commodities by considering the rise of an event coextensive to the rise of shopping, namely, modern pornography. Modern pornography, as a visual display of female redundancy, extravagance, and surplus, sets itself apart from older forms of sexually explicit representation. Considering shopping and pornography in relation to each other allows us to see how a culture produced fantasies about women's commodiousness in relation to male need.

As a noun, *shop* considerably predates the eighteenth century; the OED traces the earliest reference to the fourteenth century. However, the verb *to shop*— "to visit a shop for the purpose of making purchases, or examining the contents"—only appears in 1764. Once we recognize the ready availability of shops by the end of the eighteenth century, as well as numerous accounts of eighteenth-century consumer activity, we can safely claim that much of what is supposed to be peculiarly modern about nineteen-century consumerism was in place long before. Rachel Bowlby, for instance, citing Guy Debord, describes how "modern consumption is a matter not of basic items bought for definite needs, but of visual fascination and remarkable sights of things not found at home."[5] However, here is the West End of London, as described by John Stow, during the early seventeenth century:

> Their shops made a very gay Shew, by the various foreign Commodities they furnished with; and, by the Purchasing of them, the People of *London,* and other parts of *England*, began to spend extravagantly . . . . Some of the Wares sold by these Shop-keepers were Gloves, made in *France* or *Spain*, Kersies of *Flanders* dye, *French* cloth, or Frizado, Owches, Brooches, Agglets made in Venice or Milan, Daggers, Swords, Knives, Girdles of the *Spanish* Make, Spurs made at *Milan, French* or *Milan* Caps, Glasses, painted Cruses, Dials, Tables, Cards, Balls, Puppets, Penners, Inkhorns, Toothpicks, Silk-bottoms and Silver-Bottoms, fine earthen Pots, Pins and Points, Hawks-Bells, Saltcellars, Spoons, Dishes of Tin.[6]

If the spectacle of "remarkable sights of things not found at home" fails to distinguish later from earlier experiences of commodity, what helps to define eighteenth-century experience of goods for sale? And what accounts for the rise of shopping as a discrete form of consumer activity in the second half of the eighteenth century?[7] I will argue that the rise of modern shopping can be understood in two different ways: first, as a linguistic process, in which we can trace important changes on the level of words themselves, and second, as a cultural process, in which an evolving understanding of interior space generated new codes of behavior for retail activity. As we will see later, both of these factors had profound implications for women, since both processes entailed ideologically fraught notions about gender.

Shopping, then, appears to result from the convergence of two cultural processes that are recorded on the level of language—the evolution of commodity away from what is commodious and the evolution of luxury away from what is lascivious. This convergence of commodity and luxury can be best visualized in terms of a semiotic square, which suggests the "relation of their reciprocal presupposition."[8] The square is formed by two pairs of binary oppositions: (commodious) (not commodious) and (lascivious) (not lascivious). The first binary pair marks a movement in the term *commodity* from what is, literally, according to the OED, "commodious," what is "advantageous, beneficial, profitable, of use" or what is "convenient, suitable, or handy" toward the more modern definition of the word: "a thing produced for sale," "an item of commerce, an object of trade." According to this paradigm, the second term marks a *discontinuity* in the idea of commodiousness.[9] This binary pair suggests that, as commodity evolves, it displays a tension between what is genuinely useful and what is, regardless of actual benefit, valuable for its exchange value.

The second pair displays a related tension between two ways of thinking about *luxury*. An older way involves an understanding luxury as something entailing "lasciviousness, lust." A newer way, which takes hold sometime during the course of the eighteenth century, involves understanding the word as "the habitual use of, or indulgence in what is choice or costly" (OED, definition 4). In other words, luxury as lasciviousness slowly disburdens itself from the moralistic inclination that had associated it with the sinful indulgence of the body. Beginning in the late eighteenth century, luxury as not lasciviousness becomes "something which is desirable but not indispensable." As was the case with the first binary pair, the two terms here also mark a discontinuity: luxury as not lasciviousness does not imply the absence of but rather a shift in the concept of luxury as lasciviousness.[10]

Put together, the two binary pairs form a square in the following manner:

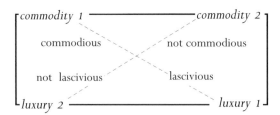

Reading diagonally gives us two continuums. The first ranges from commodious to lascivious and is consistent with an older understanding of *lux-*

ury as something that is not needed, not essential, and possibly illicit. This is the axis of "sufficiency." The second ranges from "not commodious" through "not lascivious" and approximates a more modern understanding of *luxury*. (Think of a luxury car: while not purely "commodious," neither is it "lascivious.") This is the axis of "excess."

The virtues of thinking about the evolution of commodity in this way are manifold. First, the semiotic square helps us to understand how the terms *commodity* and *luxury* depended upon each other for their definition. In its modern form *commodity* required the existence of *luxury*, just as *luxury* was meaningless without *commodity*. Second, we can understand how people conceptualized their relationship to goods in terms of several possible continuums: one object was more or less commodious; another was more or less lascivious. Some objects were more luxurious than commodious. And so on. People's conceptualization of goods, their understanding of their place in a social setting, was never static but always shifting. At the end of this chapter I will return to this square as a way of further understanding women's relationship to commodity; it is useful as well for contextualizing the appearance of modern pornography.

For the time being we notice that shopping appears to have been born at the moment when commodity and luxury converge. Thinking historically, we could say that shopping is an activity centered around the purchase of commodities that were becoming less commodious, more indulgent and habitual. Shopping—unlike marketing or other forms of buying—entails the purchase of what is "desirable but not indispensable."[11] Indeed, according to one historian, in the countryside the practice of shopping first occurred when customers went in search of three commodities in particular: caffeine products (coffee and tea), tobacco, and sugar. "The demand for [these] groceries only obtainable from abroad and not traditionally sold in the public market stimulated the mercantile community to set up country shops."[12] Only then did other commodities follow, until shops sold a wide array of goods. What is significant about these three commodities is, of course, that each was also once considered a luxury, and the adoption of each for daily consumption gave rise to its own polemic.[13] Once the practice of visiting the country shop for these no longer luxurious commodities became a familiar habit, the door was opened for other forms of consumer behavior. If the first form of mass consumption was literally dependent upon addiction, later forms of consumerism would also depend upon a pressing sense of necessity.

Within a context where consumption is more than a matter of physical need, the language that describes the compulsion to shop quickly assumes gendered overtones. In the language of trade, buyers are most often rendered feminine and submissive, regardless of their actual gender. The seller, in contrast, assumes a dominant, masculine position. Yet the dichotomy between seller and buyer threatens to collapse precisely because of its recourse to gendered metaphors: if a feminine shopper is a submissive shopper, she is also a potentially subversive shopper. As such, she is capable of interrupting the orderly flow of commerce.

Shops and Shoppers

Shopping was, then, the pursuit of particular kinds of commodities increasingly made available in a shop. A shop, however, was a special kind of indoor space. It evolved out of the changing location of consumer activity. Before the rise of modern retail, most consumers encountered goods to be purchased in markets, fairs, or exchanges. Itinerant peddlers also made goods available. However, according to two historians,

> By the end of the century, the wholesale functions once performed by the fair had long since fallen into desuetude. All that remained of the great fairs was the trade in livestock and some foodstuffs. Gone too was the packman merchant. Both had been replaced by pattern cards, circulars, and commercial travelers that allowed the shopkeeper to order goods when and as he needed them and from whomever he wished. . . . Shops, which had begun to encroach upon the trade at the fairs even in the seventeenth century, were firmly established in the eighteenth century.[1]

This shift in the location of consumer activity was matched by another important change in the idea of the market from a place to a process. Jean Christophe Agnew explains that in ancient times the market was a specific place, "a place created as much by culture as by convenience. As a threshold of exchange, the market drew on earlier rituals of passage to distance itself from the many worlds that were indiscriminately mixed in it."[2] Eventually, the space of the market became more figurative than literal. In England Agnew traces the word *market* to the twelfth century: "In its earliest usage, the word referred alternatively to the area, the occasion, or the gathering of buyers and sellers assembled within a specific time and place." By the sixteenth century the word comes to refer to "the acts of both buying and selling, regardless of locale, and to the price or exchange value of goods and services." The term becomes increasingly abstract, until, writes Agnew, "By the end of the eighteenth century, 'market' had come to imply, especially in literate circles, a boundless and timeless phenomenon."[3]

While the term *market* lost its specificity over the course of the eighteenth century, the noun *shop* became more precise, indicating a discrete indoor space with a particular purpose. Yet shops had not always been indoor spaces with particular purposes. During the middle ages, for example, shops were rooms in houses that lined the market: according to Dorothy Davis, "open-fronted at street level . . . they were house, warehouse, workroom and shop in one. Business was done with the customer standing in the street and dealing over the dressing board or counter."[4] Of course, this arrangement was partly dictated by the lack of a suitable source of artificial light; indoor spaces would have been too dark to allow the customer to scrutinize the goods, and authorities circulated to survey market processes. Some time around the end of the seventeenth century, however, the customer had begun to move indoors, as suggested by this comment from *The Compleat Tradesman* (1684): "If any chance to step in, [the shopkeeper] hath hocus tricks enough to delude them, and rarely shall they stir out (like sheep engaged in briars) but they shall leave some fleece behind them."[5] This movement indoors surely owed something to the improved manufacture of glass for windows; plate glass windows do not appear until the late eighteenth century, however. Although window displays date also from the second half of the eighteenth-century, the practice of displaying the goods on the board in spectacular fashion was much older.

Corresponding to this understanding of the shop as an indoor space was the movement toward recognizing the shop as the discrete site of consumer activity. As we know, early shops had simply been the extension of the workshop or, indeed, the shopkeeper's domicile. By the end of the eighteenth century, though, "the most prosperous tradesmen were now beginning to take houses for their families in the country, and travel in each day."[6] While this situation might not have been possible for shopkeepers of lesser means, it nonetheless marks the impetus to isolate the space of commercial trans- action from both the site of production and the home. This separation was significant, as it potentially enhanced the intensity of the sale process. As Davis points out, as long as the family lived upstairs—with only one interior staircase and no privy on the premises—customers might have been sub- jected to the sight of the family's wastes being carried out through the shop.[7] Thus the sales process could become more intense once other distractions were removed from the scene.

The tendency toward indoor shopping was matched by an interiorization of the selling process. What had formerly occurred on the outside, became, both literally and metaphorically, an interiorized phenomenon. Because no prices were affixed to goods, buyer and seller alike participated in a process of psychological "reading," each trying to assess the other.[8] The seller looked for clues about the buyer's willingness—and ability—to pay, while the buyer sought out the signs that the bargain was real, all the while seeking to convince the seller of his own ability to pay, regardless of the price. As Davis writes, "Even the simplest purchase was a cautious bargain struck between two mutually suspicious individuals. It was the customer's job to keep his end up and impress the salesman, even (or perhaps especially) an apprentice; to make it clear that he was a good judge of whatever he was about to buy and had ample means to pay for it."[9] The sort of mutual reckoning Davis describes here differs radically from the far less decorous approach of the seller at the open shop window, who might well have accosted passersby with the bawl "What lack ye?"[10] It does indeed seem to have been the case that modern interiorized processes of salesmanship could only occur after the customer had moved indoors, into the interior space of the shop.

The intimate interior of the shop eventually became very different from the openness of the market, fair, or exchange, with their public forms of barter. In the shop interactions that once occurred outside in the open space, where the rhythm and flow of the crowd allowed for a certain ease, became codified, imbued with intensified meaning. The close parameters of the shop dictated new forms of behavior for all involved. The space of the shop was a space quite unlike any other, and yet the evolution of this space was histori- cally related to other enclosed and interior spaces, where the emphasis also fell on ritualized behaviors. Though one would behave differently at the tea table, for example, both settings required proper self-discipline and demeanor. Like the participant at the tea table, the denizen of a shop was contained and subjected to scrutiny as the browser at the fair was not. Yet the scrutiny to which she was subjected was also a learned behavior, one that resulted from a careful study and consideration of the selling process. The seller learned his behavior, in other words, as much as the buyer learned hers.

A plethora of trade manuals and directories from the mid-eighteenth century testify to the urgent need to codify the practices and activities of the merchant; these texts speak to a trend toward the professionalization of selling.[11] They reflect as well a concern with disciplining unruly business activities in hopes of claiming respectability for a nascent business community. Most often these manuals offer practical advice of the most basic sort—from the location and schedule of seasonal fairs, to sample bills or accounts, to foreign exchange rates. For the young apprentice they offer such advice as how to master standard written and spoken English and information on proper forms of address.

Daniel Defoe's *The Complete English Tradesman* is perhaps the most famous of such manuals.[12] Defoe insists that the tradesman interiorize the most radical forms of self-discipline, so that he might later be able to exercise more perfect control over the entire commercial transaction. As we will see, although both men and women were sellers of goods, Defoe construes retail activity as a masculine process entailing supreme self-mastery. He begins by identifying "patience" as the most important element in the tradesman's "stock": "I mean, that patience which is needful to bear with all sorts of impertinence, and the most provoking curiosity that it is possible to imagin [*sic*] the buyers, even the worst of them, are or can be guilty of" (1:103). He goes on to provide examples of unacceptable customer behavior.

> I have heard, that some Ladies, and those too persons of good note, have taken their coaches and spent a whole afternoon in *Ludgatestreet*, or *Covent Garden*, only to divert themselves in going from one mercer's shop to another, to look upon their fine silks, and to rattle and banter the shopkeepers, having not so much the least occasion, much less the intention, to buy anything; nay, not so much as carrying any money out with them to buy anything if they fancied it. (1:104)

Still, a clever shopkeeper might catch such a shopper "in her own snare" by showing her an especially enticing piece of merchandise. Unable to resist, she might "lay out the money, whether they had it or no; that is to say, buy, and send home for money to pay for it" (1:105).

However, the key to this kind of successful selling is the tradesman's own ability to master his own emotions. He must turn himself into a machine: "A tradesman behind his counter must have no flesh and blood about him; no passions, no resentment; he must never be angry; no not so much as seem to be so" (1:103). Defoe eloquently insists upon this point. In a lengthy passage, worth citing in its entirety, he describes the painful process of emotional self-discipline to which the tradesman must subject himself, as well as the consequences that follow from this self-discipline in the shop:

> It is true, natural tempers are not to be always counterfeited; the man cannot easily be a lamb in his shop, and a lion in himself; but let it be easy or hard, it must be done, and it is done: there are men who have, by custom and usage brought themselves to it, that nothing could be meeker and milder than they, when behind the counter, and yet nothing be more furious and raging in every other part of life; nay, the provocations they have met with in their shops have so irritated their rage, that they would go up stairs from their shop, and fall into frenzies, and a kind of madness, and beat their heads against the wall, and mischief themselves, if not prevented, till the violence of it had gotten vent, and the passions abate and cool. Nay, I once heard of a shopkeeper that behav'd himself to such an extreme, that when he was provok'd by the impertinence of the customers, beyond what his temper could bear, he would go up-stairs and beat his wife, kick his children about like dogs, and be as furious for two or three minutes as a man chained down in *Bedlam*, and when the heat was over, would sit down and cry faster than the children he had abused; and after the fit was over he would go down into his shop again, and be humble, as courteous, and as calm as many man whatever; so absolute a government of his passions had he in the shop, and so little out of it; in the shop a soulless animal that can resent nothing, and in the family a madman; in the shop meek like the lamb, but in the family outrageous like a *Lybean* lion. (1:114–115)

In this way, Defoe articulates the process of self-mastery that he sees as the cornerstone of the tradesman's professionalism. He depicts the human emotions as a powerful disturbing force that has no place in the tradesman's business; he also recognizes how pent up passions will explode under other circumstances. The spectacle of an explosive father who weeps after violently abusing his family evokes a mixed response: does Defoe have more pity for the victims or the man who experiences such powerful remorse?

The entire passage operates around a series of binary oppositions, which can be summarized thus:

shop—————————versus————————home
shop	home
business	family
control, mastery	lack of control, no mastery
no emotions	emotions
self-government	violent behavior
"soulless animal" (machine)	"chained in Bedlam" (madman)

Of special interest here is the relative weight given to two specific places, shop and home (suggestively represented by "upstairs" and "downstairs"). In this analysis everything to the left bears an affinity to what has been culturally encoded as masculine, while the right is aligned with what has been culturally encoded as feminine—Western culture traditionally associates not only the home but also emotions, disruptive or explosive behavior, and even madness, with femininity.

Still, the entire binary functions paradoxically, since the purpose of the bifurcation is to produce a *lion* who can become a *lamb*. In other words, the binary incorporates a tension when Defoe situates the fiery temper of the lion under the feminized locale of home, while he aligns the meek, passive temperament of the lamb with the masculinized shop. Indeed, he explicitly writes that the purpose of bifurcating the worlds of home and business is to produce a "perfect complete hypocrite" (1:114), someone who appears to be what he is not—a domesticated, weak, and passive animal. However, his countenance will belie the depth of the passion within: the tradesman becomes a more masterful agent in mastering himself and in presenting a (false) image of meekness and passivity. He becomes, in short, a more masterful man in adopting a "feminized" countenance. Defoe writes, "When a tradesman has thus conquered all his passions, and can stand the storm of impertinence, he is said to be fitted up for the main article, namely, the inside of the counter" (1:116). Defoe's use of the preposition "inside"— instead of "behind"—is telling. He explicitly refers here to the interior space, the booth in which the tradesman sits, and yet he implicitly refers his reader to the interiorized processes, the prepsychological manipulation: all that occurred "on the inside" and that increasingly characterized the commercial transaction.

Thus Defoe's text facilitates an understanding of the importance of gender to modern retail practice. His point that the tradesman's professionalism lies in his mastery of a particular kind of masculine persona can be seen against another image, also common to the age, of the disruptive shopper. Almost always represented as a woman, this shopper brings chaos not only to the shop but to the entire commercial transaction as well. The *Spectator* offers us a depiction of such a shopper. One female china seller, alias "Rebecca," writes in to complain about a "Club of Female Rakes" who plague her two or three times a day. As she lists her complaints, it becomes clear that her agenda goes beyond bad shop behavior:

> These rakes are your idle Ladies of Fashion, who having nothing to do employ themselves in tumbling over my Ware. One of these No-Customers (for by the way they seldom or never buy any thing) calls for a Set of Tea Dishes, another for a Bason, a third for my best Green Tea, and even to the Punchbowl there's scarce a Piece in my Shop but must be displac'd and the whole Agreeable Architecture disorder'd, so that I can compare 'em to nothing but the Night-Goblins that take a Pleasure to over-turn the Disposition of Plates and Dishes in the kitchens of your housewifely Maids.[13]

The disruption she describes—merchandise displaced, order made into disorder—suggests profoundly undisciplined—and undomesticated—female shoppers. Indeed, their intention is precisely to reverse the work of a proper, "housewifely" maid who strives to keep things in their place. Akin to a nocturnal supernatural force (a witch comes to mind), these shoppers have unruly desires that make it impossible for the female china seller to discipline the retail process. One of the more interesting points about this passage is how the female seller both is and is not like the women who frequent her shop. On the one hand, class differences separate. The upper-class customers are at leisure to work out their "spleen" by shopping, but the china seller finds herself none the richer when they leave: "Lord! What signifies one poor Pot of Tea, considering the Trouble they put me to? Vapours, Mr. SPECTATOR, are terrible things; for tho' I am not possess'd by 'em my self, I suffer more from 'em than if I were."[14] The last phrase, though it explicitly refers to the trouble caused by the china ladies, introduces a curious ambiguity: does Rebecca suffer from the china ladies' vapours, or would she suffer from "vapours" that plague all women who are privileged enough to spend their days shopping? In either case, Rebecca, relatively helpless in the face of such disruptive female power, appeals to male authority to help her with the presence of the "China-women." Apparently unable to write herself, she employs her son, a schoolboy, as her secretary in order request that Mr. Spectator "admonish all such Day Goblins."

In contrast, the "masculine" tradesman constructed in the pages of a work like Defoe's is supposed to know what to do when confronted by such a presence. The mastery of his passions (an essential aspect of a larger process of self-discipline) functions strategically to masculinize his profession in the face of an attendant fear that shopping brings with it the taint of the feminine. For clearly the idea that certain aspects of retail were effeminizing persisted. For example, the *London Tradesman* defines the mercer in the following way: he is "the twin brother of the woolen draper, they are alike one another as two eggs—only the woolen draper deals chiefly with men, and is the graver animal of the two, and the mercer trafficks mostly with the Ladies, and has small dashes of effeminacy in his constitution."[15] Comments such as this one testify to an ongoing cultural concern: insistence on masculinized, disciplinary practices for business appears to have functioned to quell residual fears of a feminine component in retail.[16] Moreover, as we will see in the next section, as business is construed as masculine, the feminine presence is increasingly denigrated. Women who persist in business are characterized as prostitutes—women whose real business is to sell the body.[17]

Thus, in the modern shop, the interiorized processes of salesmanship are borrowed from preexisting ideological definitions of gender. However, while one writer finds that "the dominant ideology of feminine subjectivity in *the late nineteenth century* perfectly fitted woman to receive the advances of the seductive commodity" (emphasis added),[18] we have observed how an equally powerful ideology in the eighteenth century constructed women and men in relation to the retail process. For women there were two essential components to this construction. On the one hand, the intimate space of the shop, a space resembling other kinds of intimate domestic interiors, often facilitated both a rhetoric of seduction and the construction of a yielding and compliant feminine consumer who was made vulnerable precisely because she could be scrutinized at such close range. On the other hand, because shopping could be depicted as a disruptive chaotic activity, where retailers could be exhausted by an insatiable female desire to see without buying, women were continually viewed as powerful agents, capable of subverting the retail scene. For the retailer this meant that his livelihood depended upon the successful presentation of a masterful persona. While all sellers were not male and all buyers were not female, each participant in the retail process was assigned a gender-marked position. The seller was most often cast in the dominant, or masculine, role of the seducer and the buyer, characterized either by her malleability or by her disruptive desires, as feminine. In the parlance of the time, the buyer became the one to be "seduced" as well as mastered.

To see more clearly how the dynamics of shopping entailed gender-marked positions, we can look at three different literary scenes transpiring in shops: the first comes from Mandeville's essay "A Search Into the Nature of Society," the second from Richardson's *Clarissa*, and the third from Frances Burney's *Camilla*. Though only the last two come from novels, all three offer us fictionalized accounts of what happened when one went shopping. That is, all three offer us imaginary renderings of how the new commercial space generated social identities for men and women alike. None of these scenes is, in any simple sense, mimetic, and none has the status of "truth," yet all offer us a very true and specific understanding about the nature of commercial transaction. Mandeville describes the paradigmatic sale as the scene of seduction and psychological "penetration." Richardson and Burney depict further permutations on that paradigm. Only Burney—obviously the only woman writer here—attempts to depict the sales scene from a female point of view.

In a 1723 essay appended to later editions of *The Fable of the Bees*, Mandeville sketches for his reader the very nature of shopping. He describes how a male mercer, with privileged access to the real value of the goods, faces off the lady customer, who mistakenly believes she has the upper hand. On her way to the shop she prepares for the transaction by taking stock of her own powers: "From the Impression the Gallantry of our Sex has made upon her, she imagines (if she be not very deform'd) that she has a fine Mien and easy Behaviour, and a peculiar Sweetness of Voice; that she is Handsome; and if not Beautiful at least more agreeable than most Young Women she knows."[19] Having considered a range of possible roles, including the lover and the tyrant, she settles on being "As Amiable as Virtue and Rules of Decency allow of" (353). However, all her preparation comes to nothing, since the mercer quickly masters his customer by applying himself to her inflated sense of self-worth and flattering her tastes: "Let her say and dislike what she pleases, she can never be directly contradicted: she deals with a Man in whom consummate Patience is one of the Mysteries of the Trade, and what ever Trouble she creates, she is sure to hear nothing but the most obliging Language, and has always before her a chearful Countenance, where Joy and Respect seem to be blended with good Humour, and altogether make up an Artificial Serenity more ingaging than untaught Nature is able to produce" (353). The mercer "makes her swallow very contentedly the substance of everything he tells her" (354), and ultimately she pays exactly what he wishes her to pay, although she goes away with the mistaken notion that she has bought a bargain.

What makes this woman—like any woman—the ideal customer for Mandeville is that she is so impressionable. Her vanity and her exaggerated self-worth are the product of male flatterers. Having "no character at all," this customer can be easily addressed by the mercer, who molds her as he wishes. This lady is "between men," between those who initially flattered her and the mercer who has reshaped her in accord with his own interests. What makes the mercer the ideal salesman, in contrast, is his acute psychological insight, an insight especially attuned to the customer's narcissism: "By precept, Example and great Application he has learn'd unobserv'd *to slide into the inmost recesses of the Soul*, sound the Capacity of his Customers, and find out their Blind Side unknown to them: By all which he is instructed in Fifty other Stratagems to make her over-value her own Judgment as well as the Commodity she would purchase" (353–354; emphasis added).

The lady customer never knows what has truly transpired. Having rejected the role of lover, she thinks she has not been involved in a seduction. However, the mercer's act of sliding "into the inmost recesses of the

Soul" most resembles an amorous invasion. This seduction works especially well because the mercer gives his customer the false impression that she is always in control. As Bowlby writes, "The essential point is that the making of willing consumers readily fitted into the available ideological paradigm of a seduction of women by men, in which women would be addressed as yielding objects to the powerful male subjects forming, and informing them of their desires."[20]

Mandeville's scene is paradigmatic, then, in that it psychologizes the commercial transaction. It constructs the mercer as a masculinized person of superior insight and power, while it imagines the subject position of the shopper as feminine. Mandeville's shopper is a person of no stable identity. She is a shifting category of subjectivity, vulnerable to invasion and mastery precisely because she depends so heavily upon others for her sense of self. In this paradigm we see the rudiments for modern consumer culture, which continues to depend upon the customer's shifting sense of identity for its efficacy.

In contrast to Mandeville, Richardson's interest in *Clarissa* (1747–1748) was to locate the transcendental nature of his female heroine literally "above" the shop. It is surely no coincidence that Clarissa's last residences is a suite of rooms directly above a commercial setting, specifically, a glover's shop. Yet, while the selling process goes on directly below her, Clarissa remains entirely immune to the commodification process to which both her family—and her society—would subject her. As we will see, Richardson's use of the shop has additional significance as a commentary on the nature of the class dynamics introduced by a writer like Defoe.

Not long after Lovelace has raped Clarissa, when he first learns that she has escaped from Mrs. Sinclair's, he imagines her "fairing," that is, skipping out freely among life's various attractions, for, as he envisions, the world "is but a great fair . . . all its toys but tinselled hobby horses, gilt gingerbread, squeaking trumpets, painted drums, and so forth."[21] In the passage that follows he conflates Clarissa's imaginary movement through the market with her being on the market, as he envisions her suitors pursuing her:

> Now behold this pretty little miss skimming from booth to booth in a
> very pretty manner. One pretty little fellow called Wyerly, perhaps
> another jiggeting rascal called Biron, a third simpering varlet of the
> name of Symmes, and a more hideous villain than any of the rest . . .

ycleped Solmes pursue her from raree-show to raree-show, shoulder-
ing upon one another at every turning, stopping when she stops, and
set a spinning again when she moves—And thus dangled after, but still
in the eye of her watchful guardians, traverses the pretty little miss
through the whole fair, equally delighted and delighting. (970–971)

But at this point in the narration Clarissa is neither in the market nor on the
market. She is neither interested in the world of commodities that might
easily be available to her nor willing to participate in a marriage market that
had consistently treated her as a commodity.

As Lovelace pursues Clarissa to the Smith's, his access to her barred, he
persists in the mistaken notion that he can "buy" Clarissa by first buying the
favor of the Smiths (1209–1218). In the glover's shop Lovelace displays a
series of parodic behaviors that comment on correct business practice.
Breezing into the shop, dressed in a very fine suit of clothes (part of his wedding trousseau, in fact), attended by his servant, Lovelace—not unlike Mandeville's female shopper—imagines the dazzling impression he will make on
those in the shop. Pushing his way past Mrs. Smith, who is behind the
counter, he forces his way up the steps toward Clarissa's rooms. Once he is
finally convinced that Clarissa is not on the premises, he turns instead to the
sport of disrupting the Smith's business. Back downstairs in the shop, he sits
in the seller's alcove, which he describes as "an arched kind of canopy of
work." He mocks the pretensions of the trader who would sit there and
demands to be served. When Mrs. Smith explains she cannot serve him if he
is in her place, he decides to sell instead.

In the scene that follows the world is temporarily turned upside down;
the fine gentleman becomes the trader, the least distinguished female pedes-
trian, who has been "gaping at the door," his customer. Instead of mastering
his own passions to better master his customer, as the trade manuals had dictated, Lovelace insults her, telling her that she is "plaguy homely," and sends
her on her way. He mocks, in other words, the very self-discipline that
Defoe had identified as essential to a masculinized commercial identity. As a
gentleman, Lovelace owes his identity to birth, not behavior. He can afford
to expose the practices that enable the tradesman's mastery of his femi-
ninized customer as nothing but a game, for his livelihood does not depend
upon them.

He turns his attentions instead toward a more genteel lady and engages her attention by making a mock sale of some gloves to her footman. But, when the footman's fingers are too big to fit the gloves, he threatens to "pare" his "paws" (1212). This is the second time in this scene that Lovelace has threatened someone with a knife. A moment earlier he had also pretended that he was going to excise a few teeth from one of the Smith's employees, "dark" Joseph (1214). The idea of "pruning" here—at broad teeth or thick fingers—is suggestive, for it introduces the sadistic subtext that informs the whole scene. Lovelace's game is to "cut away" what so many others in the commercial setting depend upon—an illusion of power, thought to be held by those who have subjected themselves to a masculine form of self-discipline. Lovelace's phallic display—his talk of knives and cutting—constitutes an aristocratic challenge to a class identity in the making. As John Richetti has written, Lovelace practices a form of "aristocratic vandalism, an assertion of archaic and anarchic privilege that runs rough shod over the contractual affiliations that presumably link the Smiths and their employees like Joseph."[22]

Though Lovelace may ridicule the rituals of selling, those rituals are crucial to a class of men like "dark" Joseph. They become the means to assert a gendered identity within shifting class relations. Behaving as he does in the shop, exposing social conventions as arbitrary forms of behavior, the aristocratic Lovelace threatens to "cut through" the social fictions by which tradesman construct themselves as men. Yet his childish display is symbolic on another level: for the commercial world he aggressively mocks is also the ultimate origination of his beloved Clarissa. Richardson, having carefully established the utterly bourgeois foundations of the Harlowe family fortune, makes clear the ironic reversal that makes Clarissa Harlowe Lovelace's moral superior. Thus Lovelace's mockery of the Smith's business can also be read as displaced hostility toward the newer, threatening social mobility brought on by the incursion of the commercial class into the social scene.

Richardson's work, dating from the mid-century, shows us retail practices that are still subject to harassment by aristocratic whim. The appearance of Frances Burney's work corresponds more keenly to the full implementation of retail practice. In Burney's first work, *Evelina* (1778), published only fourteen years after the first recorded instance of the verb *to shop*, the eponymous heroine calls attention to the novelty of shopping: "We have been *a shopping,* as Mrs Mirvan calls it, all this morning to buy silks, caps, gauzes, and so forth."[23] The OED traces the gerund *shopping* to Burney's early diaries, further suggesting a historical linkage between Burney and history of retail.[24] However, it is Burney's third novel, *Camilla* (1796), that presents us with the most powerful representation of a nascent consumer culture. In one especially compelling scene at the heart of that novel, we are offered two competing versions of the female shopper. Though the novel remains committed to exploring only one kind of female consumer experience, it permits us a glimpse at another.

In book 3, Mrs. Mittin takes Camilla into Southampton under the pretense of asking shopkeepers "What there's to see in town."[25] Mrs. Mittin's real motive is, however, to scrutinize "all that was smartest, without the expense of buying anything." While, Burney tells us, this plan might have worked for Mrs. Mittin, Camilla's presence ruins the experiment, for Camilla "was of a figure and appearance not quite so well adapted for indulging with impunity such unbridled curiosity." Soon the shopkeepers notice that Mrs. Mittin never buys a thing, and that she doesn't heed their directions, going only as far as the next shop. This odd behavior, coupled with Camilla's evident distraction, generates the notion that the two women are either seeking to attract notice, deranged in mind, or engaged in some subtle kind of shoplifting, and the men observing them begin placing bets on which circumstance is true. When one haberdasher, believing Mrs. Mittin is surely insane, begins to stare at the women, they quickly leave the shop and retreat to a little bathing room. (The editor's note identifies it as a room for ladies and gentlemen to bathe by means of an artificial bottom, which could be raised up.) The men, who are waiting to have their bets resolved, speculate that the women are dividing their spoils.

Meanwhile, Camilla's sweetheart, Edgar Mandelbert, wanders onto the scene and is invited to join in the betting: he is shocked to recognize his Camilla as the object of the men's attention, and Camilla is, understandably, horrified to have Edgar see her in such a situation. At that moment "three persons, dressed like gentlemen" push their way into the bathhouse. They "boisterously" enter and force themselves upon the women. The first responds to Camilla's magisterial dismissal and makes way for her to pass out of the bathing room. The second man, Lord Valhurst, "shutting the door, planted himself against it." Camilla, now terrified, is saved from imminent peril by the third man, who, perceiving that Camilla is not what the other men believe she is, intercedes on her behalf. Lord Valhurst moves away from the door and Edgar rushes upon the scene in time to save Camilla.

The peer claims to have meant no harm, but Burney's message is clear: Camilla's inappropriate behavior in the shops, in the company of Mrs. Mittin, has clearly compromised her character and placed her in danger of the most serious kind of violation. Burney brings her heroine to the brink of a physical assault—or rape—but pulls back from the horror; indeed, she tells us that Camilla herself had no doubt of Lord Valhurst's sincere interest in her welfare. Despite this insistence, the scene leaves its chilling impact: whether intentionally or not, it unleashes a threatening sexual subtext for the heroine.

However, what is it, specifically, about the display of materialism that enhances Camilla's sexuality and encourages the men to assume that she is sexual fair game? And why do the men apparently fail to make the same assumptions about Mrs. Mittin? Leaving aside historical considerations for the moment, we might read this scene through the lens of contemporary feminist theory. For example, Susan Willis, citing Rachel Bowlby's work on the department store, describes the dizzying effect produced by the fact of the male spectator who gazes upon the woman shopping: "A woman is being looked at (consumed by the male gaze) while looking at and consuming commodities for sale. A woman's sense of self is of a self being consumed while she is herself consuming."[26] Willis thus alerts us to the easy movement, culturally speaking, from *woman as purchaser* of commodities to *woman herself* as commodity. Her work suggests that the shop frames Camilla as something "to be bought," even while, as we have seen in previous chapters, culture constructs women as the targets of commercial transaction. Indeed, to Burney's reader Camilla's status as commodity is especially obvious. Just before, Mrs. Mittin confesses that she has been spreading rumors about Camilla's status as a rich heiress (which she is not) in order to stay off Camilla's creditors. As Camilla appears on the scene with Mrs. Mittin, she becomes one of the "goods"; she is put on display as an item to be consumed.

However, this approach fails to account entirely for what transpires in Burney's shop, because the characters live in a world where a different kind of behavior is expected of women shoppers. The salesman scrutinizes Camilla and Mrs. Mittin because they do not play by the established rules of the moment. Historically speaking, the salesman would hope the two ladies would engage with him, that they would put themselves in his hands, so to speak. Mrs. Mittin's free-roving eye as well as Camilla's apparent distraction generate suspicion because, according to the convention of the day (a convention necessary when no prices were affixed to items), they are expected to pay attention to the salesman, readily yielding themselves to his control as he presents the goods and speaks of their features. Neither Mrs. Mittin nor Camilla adopts the role of the properly feminized shopper in that neither makes herself available to the salesman. Each, for her own reason, is too distracted to be mastered by the salesman. Though Camilla's appearance marks her as a lady, with the means to buy, her behavior is at odds with that appearance.

The text further suggests a vaguely salacious dimension to Mrs. Mittin's free examination of the goods. One of the onlookers describes Mrs. Mittin as "routing over everybody's best goods, yet not laying out a penny" (611). "Routing" suggests the activity of a swine, eliciting a hint of the grotesque in relation to Mrs. Mittin's easy way with the goods. *Rout* is etymologically related to *rut,* and the text hints that Mrs. Mittin is engaged in vicarious "copulation" with the goods. There is something vaguely obscene about her visual pleasure. Her looking is an illicit voyeurism for which she "doesn't lay out a penny." Mrs. Mittin, free by nature of her ambiguous class position from certain expectations, indulges herself wantonly, almost lasciviously, in a visual display designed by the shopkeeper to entice and allure, seduce and entrap. And yet she does so without any intention of actually being entrapped.

Mrs. Mittin is, of course, the direct descendent of a long line of subversive women shoppers who had plagued shopkeepers from the beginning. Like the china ladies who had disrupted the order of Rebecca's shop in the *Spectator*, or like the irritating shoppers who drove Defoe's shopkeeper to near madness, Mrs. Mittin enjoys illicit pleasures in relation to the goods. In a scenario where disciplined masculine retail practice opposes disorderly feminine desire, Mrs. Mittin threatens the established order. Because she looks without paying, she disrupts a male attempt at economic control. Labeled for a crazy woman or a thief, she is aligned with forces that resist the management of the dominant order.

The paradox of this scene is that Camilla—and not Mrs. Mittin—becomes the object of unwanted male attention. Why is it that Camilla's appearance in the shop results in her sexual vulnerability, and why doesn't the same thing happen to Mrs. Mittin? The situation is especially paradoxical in that, for the balance of this very long book, Camilla embodies Nancy

Armstrong's definition of the "new domestic woman," that self-regulating, self-conscious, and self-aware woman who learns through trial and efforts to internalize the new codes of domestic conduct." As Armstrong writes, the new domestic woman "had no material body at all." And, indeed, we are hard pressed to say what Camilla looks like, so dematerialized is she throughout the novel.[27]

One way to think about Camilla's becoming materialized is to assume a process of metonymic displacement, whereby the female consumer becomes identified with the products she consumes. In this process of displacement, projected onto a woman are the associations of the goods that surround her.[28] Although Burney does not specifically identify the contents of the shops at Southampton, we have some clues: Camilla and Mrs. Mittin are pursued by a perfumer, a haberdasher, and a linen draper. The perfumer purveys exotic scents; among other items, the haberdasher offers sundries, including items such as tortoiseshell or ivory combs; the linen draper includes textiles like imported muslin among his wares. The collective display of such merchandise brings to mind the scene in *The Rape of the Lock*, where Belinda's dressing table offers the spectacle of the world brought home:

> Unnumber'd Treasures ope at once, and here
> The various Off'rings of the World appear;
> From each she nicely culls with curious Toil,
> And decks the Goddess with the glitt'ring Spoil.
> This casket *India's* glowing Gems unlocks,
> And all *Arabia* breathes from yonder box.
> And Tortoise here and Elephant unite
> Transform'd to *Combs*, the speckled, and the white.[29]

Other earlier eighteenth-century texts, such as James Ralph's *Clarinda* (1729) or Addison's passage in the *Spectator*, no. 69, similarly attest to the range of international merchandise associated with the decoration of the female figure.

If we were to read these international commodities associatively, we can see that what they introduce, by virtue of their origin and the conditions of their obtaining, are notions of foreignness and exoticness, distance and luxury, cultural "otherness" brought home as the result of trading activity. These commodities testify to the power of English mercantile expansion; they appear as the result of British mastery of the world market as well as British domination of the peoples originally associated with the production of these goods. Items such as imported textiles or tortoiseshell combs are presences that signal absences, luxuries that appear in conjunction with a repressed narrative of England's imperial expansion, which is being illuminated by cultural historians.[30] In several accounts, it emerges as the story of how the "rape" of foreign lands also entailed the construction of a "rapable" female other, a dark sister onto whom the West was able to project an intensified corporeality.[31]

Burney's narrative initially suggests that Camilla in the shop takes on the very associations of the commodities with which she finds herself surrounded: once Camilla appears in the shop, the men are able to project a series of associations onto her body—an otherness tainted by the hint of the illicit, as well as a luxury tied to an enticing display of availability. However, while the narrative moves in the direction of this connection, it stops short of making it explicit. In the end, this novel resists any facile statement about the heroine's status in relation to the world of goods, while the novelist refuses to render Camilla the simple victim of her circumstances.[32] The narrator insists upon an essential quality, in particular, rendered as "beauty, in the garb of virtue," which grants Camilla a "primeval power" over her would-be rapists (614). Confronted by the evidence of this power, one man, Halder, recognizes the mistaken nature of his projection and moves aside to let Camilla pass.

The narrator's insistence upon the "primeval power" of Camilla's virtue—a force that ultimately protects her against male projection—provides a privileged interiority for the upper-class heroine.[33] Camilla's possession of this power distinguishes her from Mrs. Mittin. However, if Mrs. Mittin fails to possess "beauty in the garb of virtue," what she possesses instead is a labile physical body. Precisely because she already possesses this body, metonymic displacement becomes difficult; her physical identity resists projection. Camilla is initially introduced to Mrs. Mittin in the guise of a "fat, tidy, neat looking elderly woman" in a large black bonnet and a blue checked apron (423). This turns out to be a disguise. As her checked apron yields to a flounced, embroidered white muslin apron, Mrs. Mittin reveals herself as a gentlewoman. She explains, "For I keep a large bonnet, and cloak, and a checked apron, and a pair of clogs, or pattens, always at this friend's; and then when I have put them on, people take me for a mere common person, and I walk on, ever so late, and nobody speaks to me; and so by that means I get my pleasure, and save my money; and yet always appear like a gentlewoman when I'm known" (424). Possessing not one identity but two, Mrs. Mittin is embodied in the novel as Camilla is not: she is identified as a physical presence with the chameleon power to blend into her surroundings.

Mrs. Mittin is also a working woman, though the exact nature of that work is difficult to say. Recounting the range of Mrs. Mittin's employment, the narrator registers her disapproval:

> To be useful, she would submit to any drudgery; to become agreeable, devoted to any flattery. To please was her incessant desire, and her rage for popularity included every rank and class of society. The more eminent, of course, were her first objects, but the same aim descended to the lowest. She would work, read, go of errands, or cook a dinner; be a parasite, a spy, and attendant, a drudge; keep a secret, or spread a report; incite a quarrel, or coax contending parties into peace; invent any expedient, and execute any scheme. . . . all with the pretext to oblige others, but all, in fact, for simple egotism; as prevalent in her mind as in that of the more highly ambitious, though meaner and less dangerous. (688–689)

Despite the obviously censorious tone of the narration (words like *parasite, drudge,* or *spy* conveying moral condemnation), this passage nonetheless intimates what is admirable about a character like Mittin: she is adaptable and flexible in the extreme, versatile in her talents, creative in response to her society. She lives on the edges; her performance suggests what the theorist De Certeau has called "la perruque," as John Fiske explains it: "a tactical raid by the weak upon the strategy of power in the workplace."[34] While the narrator is especially censorious of Mittin's "egotism," that quality in particular distinguishes her as commodity. For, if women are traditionally commodious in relation to the needs of others, Mrs. Mittin turns this principle to her own advantage; she consciously markets herself, turning the social construction of woman as commodity to her own financial benefit.

Though the moralizing tone of Burney's narration works against the valorization of Mrs. Mittin, nonetheless Mrs. Mittin brings a subversive dimension into the narrative. Embodied as a self-promoting item on the market, she also gains the power to move through the streets, to slip across the border that separates one social world from another. As a self-defined commodity, Mrs. Mittin also gains the license to gaze, "to ogle" the goods, without placing herself within a patriarchal economy and without fear of recrimination. Thus the shop in *Camilla* houses two kinds of female subjects, two kinds of female consumers, represented by Camilla and Mrs. Mittin. If Burney is compelled to tell Camilla's story (deeming her most often as the unwitting victim of Mrs. Mittin's indiscretions), it is worth noting that Mrs. Mittin also has a story to tell. To follow Mrs. Mittin on her rounds would take us on a very different kind of shopping adventure, where women define their own worth as commodity, where pleasures are stolen and illicit.

Pornography

In making space for Mrs. Mittin's free-roving gaze, *Camilla* also gestures toward a curious historical coincidence worth further consideration: the rise of shopping and of modern pornography were roughly contemporaneous. Mrs. Mittin's easy and loose gaze not only marks her as a subversive shopper but also reminds the reader of the historical connection between the visual pleasures of consumption and the visual thrill of pornography. To move from the codification of retail practices to the production of modern pornographic discourse provides an instructive set of parallels about cultural fantasies of female commodiousness in relation to male heterosexual desire.

Although an earlier history of "writing about whores" (the literal meaning of *pornography*) certainly precedes the eighteenth century, several historians concur that a distinctly modern form of sexual representation can be traced to the second half of the eighteenth century. As Lynn Hunt explains, "Until the end of the 1790s, explicitly sexual description almost always had explicitly subversive qualities. At the end of the 1790s, pornography began to lose its political connotations and became instead a commercial, 'hard core' business."[1] Similarly, Peter Wagner notes that pornography became "an aim in itself," separate and distinct from criticism of church or state, sometime in the second decade of the eighteenth century.[2] Walter Kendrick likewise locates the modern coinage of the word *pornography* "sometime in the century between 1755 and 1857."[3] For Kendrick, that period saw a Foucauldian shift in the understanding of the meaning and purposes of human sexuality.

A number of features distinguish older forms of pornographic representation from a more modern "hard-core" pornography. In the older representation, sexuality is used to reduce the object of representation. The point of the representation is to impugn someone—or something—by connecting the subject with scurrilous bodily acts. The viewer is positioned not to identify with the subject but to pass judgment from an aloof and distant position. In short, the aim is not to titillate but to cast aspersion. Hard-core pornography, in contrast, rarely focuses on a particular political scene or setting; its subjects are drawn from a cast of "everyday" characters. Though some argue that pornographic representation degrades its subject, in fact the explicit purpose of modern pornographic representation is harder to pin down; arguably it displays the human body in ways that paradoxically privilege—perhaps celebrate—it, even while it may thematize its subjection.[4] No longer a comment on the scurrilous nature of any particular individual, modern pornography seeks to engage the viewer in an act of voyeurism. It encourages the viewer's identification, seeking to arouse sexual feelings.

I will argue here that there are good reasons for feminists to consider this coincidental emergence of a distinctly modern pornographic representation and modern retail practices. Both the discourse of shopping and modern pornographic representation offer cultural fictions about how women might be "commodious" in relation to male need. First, to reiterate, as consumers, women were subjected to a cultural construction that deemed them commodious not because of what they could produce or do, not because of what they might contribute by means of their labor, but because of their ready availability, their apparent receptivity to the imprint of consumer culture. The feminized modern shopper, positioned within the intimate space of the modern shop, subjected to the masculinized gaze of a salesman, found herself constructed as someone to be penetrated and mastered. In employing the art of seduction in order to make his sale, the salesman hoped to awaken unrecognized desires, to mold the feminized shopper into the compliant and yielding purchaser of the innumerable pleasures that only he was able to offer her. He saw himself as holding the ultimate power over her desires.

However, as we have seen, running counter to this account of power relations within retail practice was an equally powerful fact: nothing ensured that women would become the compliant subjects so envisioned by writers like Defoe or Mandeville. To the contrary, the omnipresent image of the disruptive female shopper—the many Mrs. Mittins of the world, "routing" over the goods, disrupting the retailer's control over his shop, his very composure—suggests that real women responded in a variety of ways to cultural fantasies about the nature of shopping. While tradesmen may have implemented rigid codes of self-discipline as a way of promoting the idea of salesmanship as mastery, real shoppers were often resourceful (as they continue to be today) in response to the retailer's attempt at control. They could refuse to pay the asking price, refuse to buy at all, refuse to be mastered, seduced, or penetrated by the salesman's psychological manipulations. In resisting his mastery, they simultaneously resisted his attempt to present himself as the dominant, masculine party and they resisted being cast as malleable and yielding.

The discourse of modern hard-core pornography resembles the discourse of shopping precisely in its presentation of a fiction or fantasy about female commodity. In modern pornographic representation that commodity depends not on female reproductive capacity, not on what a woman can produce, but on her ready accessibility and availability to male sexuality. In pornographic representation, as contemporary cultural critics tell us, what the woman encodes is a cultural fantasy of male desire. Leo Bersani, for one, offers us an extended version of this thesis in his reading of *Histoire d'O*. In the story, Bersani writes, "It's as if the psychology of women were a kind of structural inference from the psychology of men": "If the purest version of man's nature is fantasized as the dangerously self-assertive father of the Oedipal stage, then the essence of the other sex, already castrated in the male imagination, is a readiness to give up the self. Women's nature, in this fantasy, is to enact the desiring fantasies of men."[5]

Similarly, Linda Williams also identifies the projective nature of the male pornographic gaze. Rather than simply rejecting the representation of women's pleasure in pornography as "inauthentic," Williams points out the powerful psychoanalytic message that pornographic film images, with their obvious fetishism of the penis, convey. Like Bersani, she sees pornography as encoding a male failure to understand and represent female sexuality on its own terms.[6] Following Williams's account, we could say, then, that pornographic media reveal their own limitations most clearly at the moment when they appear to have mastered female sexual pleasure. The orgasmic delight of the pornographic female subject in film, for example, points not to her real pleasure but to a male fantasy of what her pleasure might be. At the moment when the camera concentrates on her at the expense of her partner, it negates his importance to her. Modern visual pornography offers a fantasy about what a woman's sexual pleasure might mean to her, how it might, in Williams' words, occupy, penetrate, or possess her, as the male viewer implicitly acknowledges he cannot.

Thus the rationale for making the journey from the late eighteenth-century shop to modern hard-core pornography lies in the fact that both provide important locales for projection and fantasy. More immediately, both speak, in their aggressive attempt to control female subjectivity, to a cultural anxiety about the impossibility of controlling that subjectivity. In both the pornographic scene and the shop something within the woman herself escapes cultural control. In pornography the more the woman is represented as experiencing orgasm, the more she points to the fact that her true sexual pleasure is "not there." In the shop the more the woman is subjected to the seller's penetrating gaze, and the more the seller insists upon his mastery of her desires, the more powerful is the possibility that her desires cannot be mastered or controlled. Far from neutralizing disruptive female desire, the discourses of both pornography and shopping keep that desire very much in view.[7]

I began this chapter with a definition of commodity in its evolving eighteenth-century context. The semiotic square offered an understanding of a shifting series of relations between people and their goods.

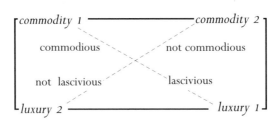

We can now see how the same square maps the position of the female body in modern pornographic discourse.[8] Commodity 1 to commodity 2 marks the movement from one cultural conception of women's usefulness to another: under the pornographic lens women are deprived of their dimension as productive useful beings. They are valued not for what they can do, but for what they can be in relation to male desire.[9] Moving diagonally from commodity 1 to luxury 1, we note that accompanying commodity 1 is an older, moralistic and blatantly misogynist discourse that identifies women as the site of lust or lasciviousness.[10] This yields, along the diagonal from commodity 2 to luxury 2, to another understanding of the female body as something closer to a "habitual indulgence" (much the way that popular thinking insists upon the "addictive nature" of pornography). Though misogyny certainly does not disappear, it takes on different forms. Thus women's commodity functions in relation to changing concepts of the luxurious. As before, the diagonal from commodity 1 to luxury 1 signals "sufficiency," an understanding of the female body that roots it in one kind of economic exchange and gives the female body one kind of value, while the diagonal from commodity 2 to luxury 2 signals "surplus"; it marks the female body as characterized by physical excess and redundancy.

Thus the semiotic square as applied to the female body provides us with another way of thinking about pornographic discourse. In particular, it demonstrates how modern pornography depended upon a crucial shift in the perception of female commodity: modern pornographic discourse could only be actualized in a climate where the concept of women's usefulness had undergone an important change. Modern pornography depends upon the possibility of women transcending the category of sufficiency in order to become part of surplus. Only when women's bodies are not actually needed do they become "desirable but not indispensable" (luxury 2); only then are they seen in relation to habit and indulgence. On the other hand, the modern definition of *luxury* as "habitual use of what is choice or costly" is also necessary to the production of pornographic technologies; such technologies only proliferate where surplus prevails and sufficiency ceases to be a concern.[11]

To see how pornography functions at the end of the eighteenth century in its distinctly modern context, consider the erotic drawings of Thomas Rowlandson, many of them made for the Prince Regent.[12] Throughout the series young female bodies, voluptuous and smooth, rounded and ample, proliferate. Though "overweight" by current standards, these bodies entice the eye and lure the voyeur into scene after scene of fleshly excess. Displayed in a series of provocative poses, these female bodies are very far from the scene of useful employment. They neither produce nor reproduce. Nude or partially clothed, they are shown dancing and swinging, tumbling down staircases, and peeing at roadside stops. Very often they are depicted in the middle of copulation itself, but they are also occasionally shown in poses that suggest that they have been sexually amusing themselves.

Yet the abundance of flesh alone does not entirely account for the sense of surplus. The actual size of the figure relative to the frame can also indicate a powerful female presence. In a drawing like "The Inspection" (*AI*), for example, the reclining female figure, torso half-turned toward the viewer, occupies nearly three-quarters of the frame, while five leering gentlemen are crammed into the upper right-hand corner of the scene. While her smooth body fills the frame, the male voyeurs jockey for space; thus her vibrant physicality eclipses theirs. While her body is drawn cleanly, with simple, elegant lines tracing her thighs, stomach, and breasts, their faces are crude, gnarled, jowled. Her sexual toys, present in the right foreground, hint at her ability to satisfy herself. Far from personifying lasciviousness, this female figure exudes good health, an overflowing of female sexual pleasure put on display for the benefit of male voyeurs who must compete for access to a view of her. While her sexuality is commodified, the male figures who leer at her are caricatured. In their smallness, with their narrow and pinched features, these male voyeurs suggest a position of inadequacy, and they provide access to the male need that produces the fantasy of female availability.

In "The Swing" (*AI*) Rowlandson omits explicit reference to the male gaze. A naked female figure, this time confronting the viewer of the picture straight on, swings out over a group of four musicians, one of whom blows his trumpet suggestively at her vulva. Again, it is the abundant female body that dominates the frame. The mood of the drawing is in fact joyous, playful, and perhaps Rowlandson is mocking the Boucher painting of the same subject.[13] In this illustration nakedness does not mean vulnerability, but a kind of absolute freedom. Similarly, in many prints Rowlandson's women appear oblivious, almost blissful in the pursuit of their own pleasure. To the extent that female sexuality is appropriated and displayed, pornographic engravings such as "The Swing" do commodify women; however, as commodity, Rowlandson's women are very often mysterious, elusive, and powerfully self-sufficient. If these women represent a cultural fantasy about female commodiousness, the message is that woman as commodity may very well be inaccessible.

In keeping with the shift toward hard-core pornography, explicit political commentary is all but absent from the erotic series; nonetheless Rowlandson does occasionally allude to two political themes in particular—religious hypocrisy and, as will be discussed later, Orientalism. The first theme is well illustrated by "Sacred Love" (*TFE* 165). Here a robed monk fondles, while holding on his lap, a naked female figure whose body is blatantly displayed for the benefit of the viewer. Participating in the same anti-Catholicism that runs rampant in the gothic novel from the period, this drawing lambastes apparent religious celibacy as a cover for a host of sexual perversions. Still, if the drawing has a "message," it is somewhat mitigated by the way it elicits the viewer's prurient interests. Because of the way the figure is displayed, the viewer is most likely to identify with the monk himself. The print is drawn to encourage the viewer's identification with the monk's pleasures in the female body. Thus the moral purpose of the print is dissipated.

Rowlandson also comments quite explicitly on the nature of female commodiousness in a number of the drawings. While female pleasure seems to exist in a world of its own, Rowlandson also draws scenes where naked women show up in the most unexpected places and become useful in the most unlikely ways. In "The Concert" (*AI*), for example, the woman's body, backed up against the male musician, both serves his sexual pleasure and holds his music across her naked backside. Yet the drawing clearly parodies the idea of her usefulness. Similarly, in "The Orchestra" (*TFE* 71) a voluptuous naked female figure plays the tambourine, as if to make her own contribution to the wild music that pours forth from the four clothed male musicians in the background.

For Rowlandson, Orientalist fantasies in particular occasion the opportunity for meditation on women as commodities. In a series representing the harem, Rowlandson borrows from racist and ethnic stereotypes of Oriental decadence to indulge the viewer's own prurient interests. In "The Harem" (*AI*), naked women, engaged in casual conversation and otherwise clearly enjoying themselves, stretch as far as the eye can see, while a man wearing a turban, seated in the foreground, surveys them. Though the scene is set in a foreign location, the women are drawn as white and European. They are depicted as relishing the fact that they are being commodified. Literally, they are a surplus commodity, with no limit to their availability. In "The Pasha" the same male figure is sexually served by four naked women. The Oriental setting, as far from the scene of British domesticity as one might imagine, thus appears to have provided the ultimate male fantasy, where women are not only abundant but ready to gratify every male wish.

The same fascination with Oriental decadence fuels one plate in the series that uncharacteristically aims for political commentary: "A Sale of English Beauties in the East Indies."[14] The "goods" referred to in the title are chiefly

"A Sale of English Beauties in the West Indies" from *Caricature Magazine*, ed. George Moutard. *Courtesy of the Yale Center for British Art, Paul Mellon Collection*

British women, though wrapped packages of "British Manufacture" also appear in the plate. In the foreground are "surgeon's instruments," pills, a carton of pornography. One version mentions *Fanny Hill* by title and includes a box of switches. The scene is a crowded dock. Men in foreign dress appraise the women who are being auctioned off. Dorothy George describes them as "courtesans," though nothing in the print explicitly identifies them as such. To the left of the drawing women who have been decreed "unsaleable" leave in tears, apparently disappointed not to be included in the auction. At the center one man resembling the pasha from the other drawing (despite the fact that a pasha is Turkish, not Indian) pokes the breast of a woman who is partially disrobed. Meanwhile, a plump, shorter man measures her height. The woman smiles obligingly and places her hand in the "pasha's." A small black boy with an umbrella hovers in the shadows of the larger white figures, an impish grin on his face. Other figures include an obese woman being weighed against a barrel that reads "lack of rupees" and a woman with her back to the viewer, whose backside is being evaluated by a man smoking a pipe. An elegant auctioneer, associated with James Christie, overlooks the proceedings.[15]

To the extent that this plate has a distinct political purpose, it falls under the category of old-style pornography. By reducing "British Manufacture" to obscene goods, pornography, s/m paraphernalia, and promiscuous women, Rowlandson attacks British mercantile practice. In that sense, sex is used to degrade a particular target. However, because the plate seeks to draw the viewer into a sexual fantasy, it also displays more modern hard-core tendencies. The plate is drawn to arouse sexual feelings at the same time that it has a serious political purpose. The woman at center, for example, is drawn to titillate the viewer. Just enough female flesh is exposed to provoke the viewer's interest. "A Sale of English Beauties" thus makes the transition from older to more modern pornography, and the female bodies in the drawing are crucial to that transition. Rendered here, once again, as surplus, as commodities linked to luxury and extravagance, the female figures at the scene are fantastically represented as commodious, as the willing participants in their own sale. Their presence thus allows for the plate to transcend its function as political commentary and to elicit the viewer's identification with sexual acts.

The small black figure exposes a xenophobic dimension in the satire, for the sale has exposed white women to the salacious gaze of a black boy, not to mention the leer of the foreign gentlemen who buy them. In one way the print is fueled by anxiety about foreignness, about the sexual license that attends traffic with foreign culture. In another way, however, it also betrays a desire for that license. Like the distorted male viewer who often inhabits the margins of Rowlandson's sexual scenes, the British viewer of this picture looks in on a scene that leaves him out of the action.

"A Sale of English Beauties" culminates the themes I have been tracing so far: here cultural fantasies about commerce mingle with cultural fantasies about female commodiousness. The impulse is to seize control of both commerce and female sexuality, to contain and regulate both. Yet the impulse to control is simultaneously rooted in a sense of being left out. Thus, if the print degrades women by implying that they are willing to sell themselves to foreigners, it also intimates that they have power as sexual agents. Women who willingly display themselves to foreign buyers subvert the power of British men. In this way they resemble the prostitutes who (as I will demonstrate in the next chapter) undermine the efforts of male businessmen.

Prints like "A Sale of English Beauties" prove the existence of a cultural fascination with commodified female sexuality. In Rowlandson, in particular, the Orientalist backdrop, attended by racist notions of the East as a place of luxury, decadence, and sexual license, fuels the fascination. Whereas Mandeville and Defoe fixated on female shoppers, Rowlandson obsesses about women as items to be shopped for. Burney's *Camilla* points to the tension between the related fantasies. Reread with Rowlandson in mind, *Camilla* reiterates how two cultural fantasies are structurally similiar. For whether women are cast as shoppers or as items to be shopped for, they function in relation to male desire as the site of projection. Burney's novel becomes the story of the heroine's struggle to circumnavigate this cultural fact.

In conclusion, we meet with a paradox: as much as modern pornography makes woman its subject, pornography is not really about women. Rather, pornography is about a cultural fantasy that is generated in response to male need. Similarly, though women and shopping have been identified with each other from at least the eighteenth century, shopping is scarcely "about" women. Instead, it too embodies a cultural fantasy generated in response to a need. In each case the more obsessive the fantasy—the more the fantasy insists on locating and controlling female "pleasure"—whether that pleasure be related to material effects or bodily pleasures—the more it testifies to a failure of control. In the subversive shopper, in the woman whose sexual pleasure lies elsewhere, something refuses to be rendered commodious. Something resists seduction, manipulation, and mastery.

In the next section, we will see how the early insistence on the tradesman's self-mastery opened up to a wider concern with the systematic implementation of masculine modes of business. In the effort to modernize business, the feminine will once again surface as a disruptive subversive force. But this time the disruption will come in the form of the prostitute: when the buyer of commodities promotes her own commodification, she disturbs the flow of business as usual.

Business

Businesswomen

Behold her then, spreading the whole tumbled bed with her huge quaggy carcase: her mill-post arms held up, her broad hands clenched with violence; her big eyes goggling and flaming-red as we suppose those of a salamander; her matted grizzly hair made irreverend by her wickedness (her clouted head-dress being half off) spread about her fat ears and brawny neck; her livid lips parched, and working violently; her broad chin in convulsive motion; her wide mouth by reason of the contraction of her forehead (which seemed to be half-lost in its own frightful furrows) splitting her face, as it were, into two parts; and her huge tongue hideously rolling in it; heaving, puffing as if for breath, her bellows-shaped and various-colored breasts ascending by turns to her chin and descending out of sight with the violence of her gaspings.[1]

This is the beginning of the end for Mrs. Sinclair, the corrupt and hardened bawd who facilitates—some even argue *forces*—the rape of Clarissa in Samuel Richardson's novel. Belford writes to Lovelace, lingering over the most minute and graphic details of her death, just as he will later write to tell Lovelace about Clarissa's death. What he describes here is not just the passing of a body, but the demise of an especially tainted, gangrenous car-cass. Mrs. Sinclair's corruption is absolute; the poison that courses through her body is both literal and symbolic. Richardson laces the passage with adjectives of size and weight—*huge, fat, broad, wide, huge* (again). These enhance the effect and render Mrs. Sinclair a force to be reckoned with. Of all the features, her mouth, so distorted it splits her face in two, gets the most attention. This mouth functions simultaneously as synecdoche for female speech—words wasted and misspent—and for female greed—inordinate desire not kept in check. It has also, of course, psychoanalytic implications.[2] But her breasts, "bellows-shaped" and "various-colored" also draw our attention. Attached to her "quaggy" carcass, they present us with a horrific image of the maternal body in decay.[3]

Within the protracted narrative of *Clarissa* this scene has several functions. Most obviously, Mrs. Sinclair must pay for what she has done to Clarissa. And she must function as moralistic complement to the paragon of virtue: Clarissa's death will be as free from taint, as removed from ugly physicality, as Mrs. Sinclair's is mired in it. With this scene, as with the death of the dissipated rake Belton, Richardson makes his point abundantly clear: only those who resist the lure of the material world will ever find true happiness. Yet the psychological energy that fuels this scene cannot be entirely accounted for by narrative purpose; something else appears to be at stake in a scene so profoundly horrific, so compellingly grotesque. In this chapter I will argue that, placed inside the larger cultural context of the mid-eighteenth century, this scene serves another function. What is important about Mrs. Sinclair is not just her spiritual corruption, her function as grotesque counterpoint to Clarissa, but also the fact that she is a *businesswoman*. The actual kind of business she engages in—trafficking in women—is ultimately less significant than the fact that she engages in business at all. Yet her particular business, prostitution, becomes, at mid-century, paradigmatic of women's business everywhere. In other words, I will argue that we can read the death of Mrs. Sinclair as ideologically motivated by cultural concerns larger than the novel.

Mid-century Britain was engaged a process of discursively constructing the world of business. That discursive construction entailed a vision of business and business practice as a masculine realm, where men, disciplined in habit, passionless in affect, controlled the flow of commerce in an orderly predictable fashion. A series of writers, from George Lillo to Malachy Postlethwayt and James Royson, were engaged in a common project of purging business from what was culturally encoded as feminine, in other words, from the physical, the irrational, the unpredictable, the unstable, and

the emotional. Arguing for a lean, well-regulated masculine form of commerce, these writers systematically align everything that is to be exorcised
from business not only with women but also with an essentialized understanding of the feminine.[4] Thus what symbolically dies with Mrs. Sinclair in
Richardson's novel is a representation of everything that business must not
be. Above all, it should not be tainted by the mortal effects of a body that is
gendered female.[5]

The discursive displacement of the feminine from business was matched
by another related phenomenon—the displacement of actual women from
the world of business. Historians, beginning with Alice Clark and Ivy Pinchbeck, and on through Peter Earle, Bridget Hill, and, more recently, Deborah Valenze, have charted that displacement, and this chapter begins with a
discussion of their work from a New Historical perspective. The task of discovering the exact nature of women's business in the eighteenth-century is
significantly complicated by constraints on what we can know and how we
can know it. After a brief historical overview of business possibilities for
eighteenth-century women, I return to key texts in which the feminine is
isolated as antithetical to business. I conclude with a discussion of one
notable profession in which both women and the feminine continued to "do
business," namely, prostitution.

The first problem in charting the displacement of women from an eighteenth-century business environment is the difficulty historians have had
ascertaining the exact nature of women's participation in the work force
from the beginning to the end of the century: where do we look to find evidence of women's business, especially when the documentation of women's
"work" is so sporadic? Historian Olwen Hufton writes, "We all know that
women in pre-industrial society worked. . . . Sense tells us that in the proto-
industrial phase their role was crucial. . . . Yet we have very little detailed
modern research bearing on the nature and importance of their labor."[6]
There are historical reasons why this is so. The accurate record of female
apprenticeships, for example, depended upon cultural perception that those
apprenticeships were somehow meaningful. Bridget Hill describes that in
the case of Coventry

> the register of apprentices covering the period 1781–1806 includes
> only men indentured. This was not because there were no female
> apprentices but because the completion of a man's apprenticeship had

political and social, as well as economic, consequences, that did not apply to women. When a man completed his apprenticeship in Coventry he qualified for freeman status, and thus for the parliamentary franchise. It was therefore important that the male apprenticeships should be carefully recorded. This was not the case for women, and may account for the far less complete records of female apprenticeships.[7]

Thus the very availability of historical records depends upon a social definition of woman as a citizen whose presence matters.

Even when apparently objective evidence speaks to us, it may only tell part of the social reality. Documents like *A Complete Guide to All Persons Who Have Any* TRADE *or* CONCERN *with the City of London and Parts of Adjacent London* would seem to provide the basis for a rudimentary statistical analysis.[8] Out of approximately four thousand names (fifty-one pages of approximately seventy-eight names per page), not more than fifty names are identifiably female. However, texts like this give a false sense of security. The legal construction of a woman as a feme covert probably obscured the participation of many women in what may have been a family businesses. As Peter Earle explain, "under common law, it would . . . . clearly have been impossible for a wife to run a business independently of her husband; the most that she could do was to assist him in his own business as his servant." Thus, it would be impossible to know how many married women were actually engaged in business in a climate where they had no independent legal or economic standing. It is quite possible that many of the male names recorded in the *Complete Guide* tacitly record a wife's business as well. The few female names in the *Complete Guide* most likely refer us to exceptions, situations in which a widow inherited her husband's business or, even more rarely, situations in which a wife had somehow managed to keep her "separate estate."[9]

Despite the paucity of evidence and the difficulties of interpretation, a consistent narrative about the nature of women's business in the eighteenth century does exist. Most modern historians follow the basic outline of a story first told by Alice Clark in *Working Life of Women in the Seventeenth Century*. Clark begins by distinguishing three kinds of production: domestic industry (where goods are produced exclusively for the family, not exchanged), family industry (where the family is the unit for the production of goods sold or exchanged), and capitalist industry (where owners of capital control production and pay men, women, and children wages.)[10] Her thesis is that, in the gradual movement from the first to the third form of production, women, across all classes, lost economic ground. Whether they belonged to the "capitalist class," or whether they worked in agriculture, textiles, trades, or professions, women experienced a loss of economic independence, finding themselves disenfranchised where they had formerly been integrated into the labor force. In addition, Clark argues that the period from the late seventeenth to the eighteenth centuries saw a radical shift in the concept of women's work, as the home was no longer the major site of production. According to Clark, then, during the eighteenth-century women had fewer and fewer opportunities to "do business" in a culture where women's work had been redefined.

Most historians writing after Clark concur with her findings. For example, although Bridget Hill qualifies Clark's terms, she too sees profound economic changes in the eighteenth century, changes that corresponded to the reorganization of agriculture and manufacturing: "Women on the whole were being pushed toward what were called the less 'skilled' work and tasks." She concludes, "In the eighteenth century as strictly defined, there seems little doubt that women lost out as far as opportunities for work are concerned."[11] Similarly, Deborah Valenze spells out in detail the ways in which many forces contributed to the loss of skilled women's work. For example, in dairying the shift to a market economy, controlled by male managers intent on "dairying for profit" through the implementation of a written, scientific, and "rational" approach, meant the belittling of women's traditional participation. In spinning "what had once been a ubiquitous, domestic industry became isolated within certain regions, specialized according to new categories of skill, and firmly structured according to gender. The new system subordinated ordinary women in every instance."[12]

Still other historians query the role of the historians' own value system in the process of historical evaluation. Maxine Berg, for example, warns against "ahistorical assumptions of static structures which entail unidirectional accounts of women's subordination." She argues, "the household economy as it has been understood is a myth. But dissected as a changing part of a dynamic process of industrial and capitalist growth or decline it can help reveal undiscovered directions and possibilities."[13] Thus Berg suggests that current assumption about work, community, and the place of family within the means of productions can color our ability to discern objectively coherent patterns of labor and to understand the nature of women's business. Similarly, Keith Snell (whose work Berg employs) cites the tendency of earlier historians to interject their "own sentiments on the proper domesticated roles of women in the family," sentiments that can effect not only the conclusions a historian draws but also the evidence for which she searches.[14]

Another problem in historiography occurs when historians confuse what may have been true with what people came to perceive as being true. Similarly, people's notions of what ought to have been facts are conflated with actual facts. This problem appears both in "purely" historical research and in cases where various kinds of literary texts are offered as historical evidence. For example, in an essay entitled "The Female Labour Market in London in the Late Seventeenth and Early Eighteenth Centuries" Peter Earle attempts to gather objective data in support of prevailing assumptions about women's participation in the labor force by turning to depositions of female witnesses before the London church courts. Yet, by his own account, the information provided by such witnesses may have been distorted by other considerations: "Naturally, discretion meant that the whole truth was not likely to be disclosed to the registrar of the court, despite the awe-inspiring surroundings and the frequent reminders of the final resting place of those who committed perjury. No one, for instance, said that she gained her livelihood from prostitution, though other witnesses claimed that more than one of the sample was a common whore or the mistress of a bawdy house."[15] In this surprising aside Earle calls attention to a key problem: the women whose life records provide him with historical evidence appear to have been engaged in a narrative process of self-creation. Responding to their surroundings, they may have created the stories they felt the circumstances warranted. This is not to say their depositions were untrue (and, indeed, some of their testimony certainly was true.) Rather, the value of these depositions may be that they record what women, facing the intimidating authority of an ecclesiastical court, perceived as the *appropriate* truth of their business.

Similarly, we need to distinguish carefully between types of documentation: while apprenticeship records offer material for statistical analysis, treatises like *The London Tradesman* are ideologically motivated. Less the record of historical fact about women in business, mid-century trade manuals are marked by polemical purpose, written to persuade or influence, convince or induce. They are not the key to a historical understanding of the period but to how an age discursively constructed its understanding of itself. The point is that such texts cannot be mistaken for mirrors of a static, social reality.

Such documents are most valuable when viewed as evidence of a particular truth the writer would like us to embrace.

Nonetheless, the confusion between what people argued to be true and what might have been true is significant. An Althusserian definition of ideology helps us to recognize that a set of beliefs can have the force of reality, if people act on the basis of those beliefs.[16] Thus, when one is seeking the historical truth about women's business in mid-century Britain, it is highly instructive to scrutinize texts like trade manuals as important records of the "imaginary relation" of a particular population to the "real relation" in which they lived. Reading such texts against each other, we discover gaps and contradictions that become the sign of an ideological purpose—namely, the discrediting of the idea and the practice of the eighteenth-century businesswoman.

Three examples of manuals from the period are *A General Description of the Trades Digested in Alphabetical Order* (1747), R. Campbell, *The London Tradesman* (1747), and "The Tradesman's Dictionary" in *The General Shop Book; or, The Tradesman's Universal Director. Being a Most Useful and Necessary Compendium to Lie Upon the Counter of Every SHOPKEEPER, Whether Wholesale or Retail, in Town or Country* (1753).[17]

According to the subtitle of *A General Description*, the author's mission is to provide information by which "Parents, Guardians, and Trustees may with greater Ease and Certainty, make choice of TRADES agreeable to, the Capacity, Education, Inclination, Strength, and Fortune, of the YOUTH under their care." Unlike other writers who address themselves less specifically to the issue of gender, this author is quite precise about what trades are appropriate for girls. Among those trades to which he claims girls can apprentice are bodice making, button making, hatband making, hoop petticoat making, mantua making, and millinery. Women could also find employment (though no apprenticeship seemed to be necessary) as broom makers, cap makers, fine drawers (needlework on woolen cloth), lacemakers (especially in the midland counties), pin makers, quilters, silk throwers, and upholstery needleworkers.

The first notable point about this list of possible apprenticeships for girls is its brevity. Comparing it with a list of parish apprenticeships in the southern counties, complied by Keith Snell in *Annals of the Laboring Poor*, we find the list in *A General Description* somewhat circumscribed.[18] Why not apprentice girls to be butchers or bakers or tailors, possibilities suggested by Snell's data? The answer lies in class difference: parish officials, eager to turn indigent girls into productive citizens, may have worried less about whether an occupation seemed "ladylike," whether it stayed within class-bound, socially prescribed definitions of gender. The concern with promoting ladylike employment may also explain why *A General Description* fails to recommend that girls be apprenticed as goldsmiths or pewterers.

Moreover, the division of labor this writer specifies is arbitrary, to say the least. He cites the profession of embroidery (which one might assume to be open to women) as "a very ingeneous Business, and fit for Lads that have some good Eye-sight and [are] not over burdened with strength" (39),[19] yet he perceives the art of "fine-drawing"—needlework on wool—as suitable for women (90). While he claims women can make thread or bone lace, he sees men alone as making the more profitable "woolsted-lace" for furniture and coaches or gold and silver lace for clothes and hats (127). While hoop petticoat making is viewed as appropriate for girls, a small number of male hoop petticoat makers make far more money: "About 20 pounds will make a Mistress of [the female apprentice]; not but there are several Man dealers in this Way likewise, who employ some Scores, nay hundreds of Pounds" (117). And stay making—a profession that required access to the most intimate circle of women's lives—remains an exclusively male province: "Fifty pounds will set up a Master, who may live very handsomely, if he can but get into a good knack of fitting and pleasing the Women" (200). This situation leads Campbell to comment, "I am surprized the Ladies have not found out a way to employ women stay-makers, rather than trust our sex with what should be kept as inviolably as Free-Masonry."[20]

By 1747 *A General Description* effectively reduces the opportunity for girls going into business to two trades: mantua making and millinery. The first is described as "a very extensive trade. . . . It is reckoned a genteel as well as a profitable Employ, many of them living well and saving money."

> They take Girls and young female Apprentices (who must work early and late as Business calls) with whom they have from five to twenty Guineas, according to the Degree of their Business, which with some is very large. As to Journeymen, they have generally seven or nine shillings a Week, and to make a Mistress, there is little else wanting than a clever Knack at cutting out a fitting, handsome Carriage, and a good set of Acquaintance. (134)

By way of contrast, the author reckons it would cost twenty pounds to apprentice one's son to a pewterer. A journeyman would make fifteen, eighteen, or twenty shillings a week, and five hundred pounds would be needed to set up. A boy could be apprenticed to a saddler for twenty pounds or more; as a journeyman saddler he would make from fifteen to twenty shillings a week, while a setting up cost one hundred pounds. Imagining comparable expenses (or less) for establishing a young woman in this trade, this writer is confident that she too can make an independent living.

Millinery is also, according to the same writer, "a most genteel Business for Young Maidens that are Proficient at their Needle, especially if they be naturally neat, and of a Courteous Behaviour." However, this is an expensive trade in which to establish one's daughter; she cannot be apprenticed to "a better one for less than twenty or thirty guineas." To set up shop requires three hundred pounds; but a diligent, sober Woman, with a "good set of Acquaintances" can do it for less" (149–150).

Despite this writer's reassurances, other trade manuals from the same period offer a different account of both the money to be made and the status of these "ladylike" trades. Discrepancies arise as soon as one consults *The General Shop Book*. This text describes hoop petticoat making as "one of the most laborious employments women exercise." It fails to find mantua making a lucrative profession, explaining that "some of [the women in the profession], who have a large acquaintance among people of condition, live handsomely, but most of them can barely live. And this is the case of almost every profession carried on by women."[21] Even a milliner, as a journeyman, "does not earn more than four or five shillings a week, and cannot set up well without one hundred pounds." What, then, was the "reality" faced by the young woman who wished to go into business for herself? Here it can only be said with certainty that she contended with powerful competing voices, which both encouraged and discouraged her, which simultaneously told her that she would be well-served by establishing herself in a ladylike trade and that she would be little better than a prostitute for doing so. These competing voices were a sure indication of an ideology of gender in the making, one that had yet to settle upon a coherent interpretation of woman's role.

Among the most vociferous of the voices against women in business is that of R. Campbell in *The London Tradesman*, which denigrates every profession that wins approval in *A General Description*. Campbell sarcastically traces hoop petticoat making to Semiramis and the Queen of Sheba, intimating that he sees the profession within a misogynist history.[22] He sneers: [Hoop-pet-ticoats] are chiefly made by women: They must not be polluted by the unhallowed hands of the rude male. . . . A Mistress must have a pretty kind of Genius to make them fit well and adjust them to the Reigning Mode, but in the main it is not necessary she should be a witch" (211). Mantua makers and milliners alike are virtually nothing more than prostitutes:

> The vast Resort of young Beaus and Rakes to Milliners' Shops exposes young creatures to many Temptations, and insensibly debauches their Morals before they are capable of Vice. . . . Nine out of ten young Creatures that are obligated to serve in these Shops are ruined and undone: Take a Survey of all common Women of the Town, who take their Walks between *Charing-Cross* and *Fleet-Ditch*, and, I am persuaded, more than half of them have been bred Milliners, have been debauched in their Houses, and are obliged to throw themselves upon the Town for want of Bread, after they have left them. Whether then it is owing to the Milliners, or to the Nature of the Business, or to whatever cause it is owing, the Facts are so clear, and the Misfortunes attending this Apprenticeship so manifest . . . it ought to be the last shift a young Creature is driven to. (208–209)

This passage is both permeated by essentializing notions of gender and fueled by propagandistic assumptions about the nature of business versus home, public versus private. Campbell seems to assume that the debauchery of innocent milliners is the *inevitable* result of their placement in an environment where men have access to them. Lickerish men are driven by their lusts, compelled to prey on the next available victim. While the issue might equally be the reform of men who sexually harass working girls, Campbell focuses instead on keeping the women away from the men. If the male sexual appetite is indeed so threatening, women do best to isolate themselves from it. Their ultimate recourse is to stay away from the business world.

Campbell envisions the millinery shop as the last stop before the streets. He implicitly makes home the environment where women are protected from the sexual impulses of men. The problem with the milliner's shop is that it is an imperfect house. The suggestion here is that, once a woman opens her *house* to the public, she makes herself sexually available. In a real house a lady would not sell. In a real house a woman is protected against the debauchery of rakes (or so the logic seems to go). True domesticity, in contrast to the world of business, is depicted as enclosed, insular, protected from the salaciousness of the business world. The proper lady finds her protection from sexually predatory men inside a real house, and she eschews all other kinds of houses.

Campbell's dire predictions deny women the opportunity for economic independence. What passes for gentility in *A General Description of the Trades*, the possibility of a refined yet lucrative profession, is redefined as sexual promiscuity. Loose morals come with the trade or perhaps they are the nature of women's business. Indeed, Campbell inadvertently puns on the very notion of business as "intercourse." Though technically *business* as a euphemism for sexual intercourse was obsolete by the mid eighteenth-century, Campbell's portrait of the milliner reduces her business to one thing alone: sex.[23] John Cleland appears to have had the same thought in mind: in *Memoirs of a Woman of Pleasure* Fanny Hill describes how a millinery shop was "the cover of a traffic in more precious commodities." The three young women, "very demurely employ'd on millinery work," are actually prostitutes who have been "train'd up with surprising order and management, considering the giddy wildness of young girls once got upon the loose."[24]

Even Frances Burney helps to perpetuate the stereotype of the wanton milliner in *The Wanderer*. Though her milliners are not actually engaged in the business of selling their bodies, they are nonetheless prey to fantasies of their own marketability, albeit through marriage. As Burney's heroine Juliet begins her career in the milliner's shop, she notes with some sympathy the miserable and unfair conditions of the shop: "The goods, which demanded most work, most ingenuity, and most hands, were paid last, because heaviest of expense; though for that very reason, the many employed, and the charge of materials, made their payment first required." Then, "her compassion for the milliner and the work-women somewhat diminished," writes Burney, "for she found that their notions of probity were as lax as those of their customers were of justice; and saw that their own rudeness to those who had neither rank, not fortune, kept pace with the haughtiness which they were forced to support, from those by whom both were possessed." Cheating their customers whenever possible, the milliners take advantage of customer ignorance to turn a profit. While Burney has little sympathy with capricious and idle rich customers, she faults the milliners themselves from not exercising greater caution in the presence of predatory young gentlemen:

And though, from race to race, and from time immemorial, the young female shop-keeper had been warned of the danger, the folly, and the fate of her predecessors; in listening to the itinerant admirer, who, here to-day and gone tomorrow, marches his adorations, from town to town with as much facility, and as little regret, as his regiment; still every new votary to the counter and the modes, was ready to go over the same ground that had been trodden before; with the fond persuasion of proving an exception to those who had ended in misery and disgrace, by finishing, herself, with marriage and promotion.[25]

Thus Burney—like Elizabeth Gaskell in *North and South*—imagines the perspective of the working girl from the vantage point of the respectable middle class. The antidote to the seductions of the work place—offered by a woman not herself in the workplace—is a solid dose of class identity: remembering who you are and the unlikelihood of social mobility through marriage is the best way to stay out of trouble.

Campbell describes mantua makers as being in a similar situation to that of the milliners: "Their want of Prudence and general Poverty has brought the Business into small Reputation" (227). While they are subject to men's sexual advances, they are also victimized by their own natures, which provoke them to disregard "natural" authority and to disrespect familial and social hierarchy: "In short, nothing can properly save them from falling but their Pride, which the Servile Condition of Journeyman too often humbles."

> [Mantua makers] ought to watch their Motion, and assist their unexperienced years of good Advice, and never think of themselves as discharged of their Parental Duty, till they have settled them in the World under the Protection of some Man of Sagacity, Industry, and Good-Nature; a Woman is also under Age until she comes (in the Law Phrase) to be under Cover. A Youth may be set a-float in the World as soon as he has got a Trade in his head, without much Danger of spoiling, but a Girl is such a tender, ticklish Plant to read, that there is no permitting her out of leading-strings till she is bound to a Husband. (228)

Referring to the construction of the feme covert, Campbell reminds his readers of the inherent weaknesses of the female sex. The double standard here is overwhelming: Campbell ignores a common cultural theme from his day, that of the "idle *male* 'prentice," most graphically illustrated in Hogarth's series "Industry and Idleness." He makes women alone into infantilized dependent beings who cannot live without constant surveillance. By the end of the century this view of woman as feme covert would also by employed by those seeking to promote the idea of the male breadwinner. Late eighteenth-century classical economists would codify the notion of a male head of household, while organized male laborers would also present themselves as the sole providers for their families. Eventually, the identity of the working woman would disappear, in Deborah Valenze's words, "behind the collective image of the dependent family."[26]

While *The London Tradesman* insists that it is bad for women to be in businesses of their own, George Lillo's play, *The London Merchant*, implies that it is bad for women to be involved in men's business of any kind.[27] At the heart of this didactic drama is a vision of the world of business as a perfect homosocial network. In the middle of the play Thorowgood urges Trueman to study business "as a science" and note

> how it is founded in Reason and the Nature of Things—How it promotes Humanity, as it has opened and yet keeps up an Intercourse between Nations far remote from one another in Situation, Customs, and Religion; promoting Arts, Industry, Peace and Plenty; by mutual Benefits diffusing mutual Love from Pole to Pole. (3.i)

Business here is the "good mistress," the rational and fair promoter of intercourse among men. It brings men together and facilitates understanding.[28] However, in the play what disrupts the harmonious vision is Millwood, the temptress and evil mistress. An early scene in act 1 establishes that Millwood plans to win the attention of the apprentice George Barnwell from his uncle, master, and friend, that is, from the homosocial network in which he is happily situated. When she asks him about love, he speaks of Trueman, his closest friend, explaining, "We live in one House, and both serve the same worthy Merchant" (1.v). Millwood's goal, then, is to entice Barnwell from the house in which men live so amiably together and to employ him for her own sinister purposes.

The topic of the apprentices and the women who tempt them is a common preoccupation throughout this period. Campbell states most succinctly, "An Apprentice is never completely miserable till he has got a wife"

(315). Defoe had more elaborate reasons why apprentices—and even tradesmen—must not marry too soon. A wife will inevitably lead the young man to incur heavy expenses, even before the apprenticeship is over. The married apprentice "is driven to terrible exigencies to supply this expense; if his circumstances are mean, and his trade mean, he is frequently driven to wrong his master, and rob his shop, or his till for money, if he can come at it; and this, as it begins in madness, generally ends in destruction; for after he is discover'd, expos'd, and perhaps punished, and the man is undone before he begins."[29] While it is reasonable to assume that a married man incurs debts that a bachelor would not, Defoe exaggerates the danger of marriage, intimating that a wife's inclination toward spending is a moral disease for which the husband will pay. Take the wife as evil influence away, he seems to suggest, and the apprentice would continue to behave morally.

Lillo's highly effective drama economically develops Defoe's theme, enlarging the idea that the apprentice's inordinate desire comes from the outside and is embodied in the form of a woman. Millwood is so wicked that her own best friend does not approve of her behavior. She describes Millwood's tactics as a removal of Barnwell's virtues, a metaphoric emasculation that leaves him powerless: "So! She has wheedled [Barnwell] out of his Virtue of Obedience already, and will strip him of all of the rest, one after another, til she has left him as few as her Ladyship or Myself" (1.v). Even the paragon Thorowgood feels himself endangered in Millwood's seductive presence. He wonders, "How shou'd an unexperienc'd Youth escape her Snares? The powerful Magic of her Wit and Form might betray the wisest to simple Dotage, and fire the Blood that Age had froze long since. Even I, that with just Prejudice came prepared, had, by her artful Story, been deceived, but that my strong Conviction of her Guilt makes even a Doubt impossible" (4.xvi). Barnwell, in contrast, is an easy conquest, and Millwood quickly persuades him first to steal from his master, then ultimately to kill his uncle.

Thus in *The London Merchant* the character Millwood becomes the projection and externalization of what might have been a psychological struggle within the apprentice himself. In real life unequal power relations or an exploitative economic arrangement might have "tempted" a disaffected apprentice to stray from the path. Youth often rebel in response to what they perceive as the hypocrisy of their elders. Though Lillo would have his audience believe that evil women are the prime source of the disloyalty among apprentices, in fact other issues—such as the uneven temperament of the master or the unfair conditions of the work—would have been stronger motivations for errant behavior. For Lillo, Millwood personifies Barnwell's desire, but she is also the essence of a malignant femininity, the very opposite of the good daughter Maria Thorowgood whose love Barnwell ignores.

Lillo allows Millwood to defend herself by defining woman as "an imaginary being," "an Emblem of thy [the male's] cursed Sex collected—a Mirrour, wherein each particular Man may see his own Likeness and that of all Mankind" (4.xviii). This statement suggests that Millwood has no life independent of the male characters' psychology. As a mirror, she does not exist except as the space onto which the male characters project their anxieties. And Millwood *is* mirror to Thorowgood in particular, especially in her rivalry with him for the body and soul of Barnwell. While Thorowgood is the "good capitalist" who sees trade as a means of promoting world peace and harmony, Millwood identifies herself as the ruthless imperialist. She gloats, "I would have my conquests compleat, like those of the *Spaniards* in the New World; who first plunder'd the Natives of all the Wealth they had, and then condemn'd the Wretches to the Mines for life, to work for more" (1.iii). Her function as evil twin or double to Thorowgood in this homosocial drama helps to explain why the plot is so unrelenting in its presentation of her evils. She must be sacrificed for Thorowgood to reclaim Barnwell, as the plot moves to expel what might otherwise taint transcendent relations among men. Millwood is unrepentant to the end, while Barnwell is returned to the bosom of homosociality. When Thorowgood offers to embrace Barnwell just before his execution, he exclaims, "Never! never will I taste such Joys on Earth; never will I so sooth my just Remorse" (5.v). Still, he finds great comfort in the embrace that follows. Renewed contact with Thorowgood saves him and is the sign of his repentance and forgiveness. Business—the ideal community of men who trust primarily each other—is purged from an alien, insinuating feminine presence. Millwood is taken to the gallows on her way to hell.

While Lillo's work enhances the notion of business as homosocial network, works like *The British Mercantile Academy* by Malachy Postlethwayt and James Royson proselytize for those attributes facilitating male bonding.[30] Regularity and self-discipline become the cornerstone of a mercantile ethos uniting a range of men, from (according to the authors) gentlemen who have earned their clerkships to sons of American planters, from those who chose to carry on foreign trade to those who "expect to share in the government"

(45). As the authors claim, "This is a good general education, a course of regular study, and genius of familiar explication, that fits men for the rational and methodical forging of others" (7). The text consistently emphasizes what should be "regularly" and "methodically" communicated (8). It privileges the counting house as the site of learning, so that "all that is transacted" will not be "no more to him than a regular confusion, who is disqualified to view the connection of the whole, with an eye of understanding" (10). Because the counting house is the place where volume is controlled, where proliferating numbers yield to mastery and calculated order, he who has learned its management also learns to assign everything its proper place.

The lessons of regularity, discipline, and control are extended to the merchant's speech. No idle chatter or easy conversation should absorb his time. Instead, the authors write,

> we have pitched on well-regulated evening conversations as an exercise the most natural, and best accommodated to our purpose. Our subjects of *debate* and *reasoning*, will be the various remarkable causes relating to the negotiation of *bills of exchange*; and curious points that regard *insurances, charter-parties, bottomrees* [a contract, like a mortgage], *baraties* [fraud], *averages, demurrages, bankruptcies*; and the like kind of occurrence, which arise in the course of practical business and which will afford a wider field of improvement, in matters of real use. (36; author's emphasis)

While bottomrees, baraties, and demurrages may not be everyone's choice of scintillating topics, this kind of conversation is designed to serve a purpose: to keep the mind focused and disciplined and to provide the opportunity for a kind of mental exercise. It is also designed to prevent the mind from following unproductive (or even worse—possibly wanton) trains of thought. Last, this kind of conversation promotes the idea of an elite community. Those not familiar with the jargon (and the authors seem to take a particular relish in tossing terms around) certainly cannot participate.

If the emphasis on discipline and order, on regularizing both the mind and the body of the merchant, seems reminiscent of Foucault's docile body, we can also think about it another way. For what is at stake in this discussion is mastery over mutability, control over what threatens to be changeable, unpredictable, or unstable in human life itself. The authors of *The Mercantile*

Academy assure their readers that the merchant is an especially resilient subject who cannot be brought down by misfortune:

> Merchants, it is true, have no exemption from those casualties, to which the whole human species is liable; yet, in the way of trade, these are often balanced, by prosperous contingencies. When it happens otherwise, the really unfortunate scarce ever want succor in distress. Even, when misfortunes have proceeded from unhappy mistakes, in point of conduct; yet whether neither integrity, and skill have been wanting, such rarely fail to rise again, in some channel of business or other. (57)

The fantasy here is to rise like the phoenix, to be capable of endless renewal or rebirth, regardless of the circumstances. However, to the extent that the human condition is characterized by mutability, and to the extent that the mortal body is ultimately not renewable, this discourse offers a poetic fantasy. Subject to the laws of nature, the human body resists the very mastery that a mercantile discourse attempts to exert over it.

Thus texts like *The London Merchant* or *The Mercantile Academy* perform a specific kind of cultural work. Circulating in a social and economic climate, where actual women are being forced out of work, such texts reinforce the idea that not only women but also the *feminine* has no place in the world of business. Writers like Lillo or Postlethwayt and Royson do not merely shore up a (socially constructed) male ethos, celebrating "masculine" virtues in the process; they implicitly isolate and denigrate what is culturally encoded as feminine.[31] If business habit must be disciplined, regularized, and resistant to mutability, it cannot be wanton, irregular, or inconstant. If the impulse of mercantile discourse is toward the denial of mortality, then merely mortal practice will never suffice.[32]

A number of theorists—ranging from Ernest Becker to Dorothy Dinnerstein, from Mary Russo to Gail Paster—have shown that wantonness, irregularity, and inconstancy have more often been associated in Western culture with the female body.[33] Through both psychoanalytic and cultural methods these writers allow us to recognize the manner in which the *female* body has historically borne the weight of cultural ambivalence about mortality. In the context of the discursive shift I have described, these theorists help us to recognize how the grotesque female body, readily available and encoded within a misogynist tradition, would have been a convenient target for those promoting the vision of transcendent mercantile practice. Thus, though a character like Mrs. Sinclair in *Clarissa* is obviously a stereotype—a flat undeveloped character serving a baldly polemical purpose—she also carries additional significance: the more that the female presence in business is denigrated through portraits like hers, the more that the male presence seems both necessary and imperative.

The discursive process I have been tracing speaks to the multiple constructions of woman: she might be deemed the purchaser of commodities, the fantasy agent of consumer transaction, or she might be the commodity herself, the equally fantastic object of the pornographic eye. According to the modern understanding of business, she might also be both the agent and the object of consumption, but only when she operated as the ostracized prostitute. The discursive construction of business is structurally similar to the discursive construction of both the tea table and shopping. All three processes involve paradox; all three ultimately confront a feminine presence that proves most resistant precisely at the moment when it seems most under control. In business the prostitute is the exorcised feminine; she testifies to the power of men to exclude women from (legitimate) business, while carrying on business herself. In the next section we will see how the definition of business as masculine had further implications for the definition of the female body and the space that was to contain it.

Prostitutes

Though Richardson relies upon stock notions of the bawd in his portrait of Mrs. Sinclair, his best imagery is reserved for moments when her business is threatened.[1] At such times in the narrative Mrs. Sinclair becomes an especially horrific representation of a business interest gone awry:

> The old dragon straddled up to [Clarissa], with her arms kemboed again—her eye-brows erect, like the bristles upon a hog's back and, scowling over her shortened nose, more than half-hid her ferret eyes. Her mouth was distorted. She pouted out her blubber-lips, as if to bellows up wind and sputter into her horse-nostrils; and her chin curdled, and more than usually prominent with passion. (883)

Occurring shortly before the rape, this scene records Clarissa's refusal to enter Mrs. Sinclair's house once more, her terror in the face of Mrs. Sinclair. But Mrs. Sinclair's anger is fueled by Clarissa's behavior, which she feels will cast doubt upon her reputable business; "And what, pray, madam, has *this* house done to you," she bullies Clarissa, fearing that she will compromise the reputation of her business. If, as one critic suggests, it is Lovelace's job to bring Clarissa into the trade, to break her in, so that she can also turn a profit for Mrs. Sinclair,[2] then Mrs. Sinclair's anger is also motivated by the real fear that she will lose a valuable commodity. Her livelihood is at risk.

In fact, Mrs. Sinclair's business, her respectable and reputed house, resembles many other thriving houses of prostitution in mid-century Britain. Some of these were memorialized, in satiric (and hyperbolic) fashion, in *Nocturnal Revels, or the History of King's-Palace, and Other Modern Nunneries, Containing their Mysteries, Devotions, and Sacrifices*.[3] To read a text like *Nocturnal Revels*, a work so obviously directed at a different audience from Richardson's polite readers, is to embark on a different sort of journey into London's sexual underworld. Nonetheless, both *Clarissa* and *Nocturnal Revels* take as their subject the nature of the bawd's business. While Richardson's text deploys horrific animal metaphors that repulse and convey notions of brutality, *Nocturnal Revels* jovially suggests that the sex trade is both healthy and lucrative. Indeed this perspective was born out by the comments of at least contemporaneous traveler, who wrote about prostitution in London:

> In the parish of Mary-le-Bone only, which is the largest and best peopled in the capital, thirty thousand ladies of pleasure reside, of which seventeen hundred are reckoned to be house-keepers. These live very well, and without ever being disturbed by the magistrates. They are indeed so much their own mistress, that if a justice of the peace attempted to trouble them in their apartments, they might turn him out of doors; for as they pay the same taxes as the other parishioners, they are consequently entitled to the same privileges.

This latter notion of a thriving well-managed business is perhaps what inspired the writers of the recent PBS version of *Clarissa* to portray Mrs. Sinclair as a slim attractive widow, despite Richardson's indications to the contrary. The eighteenth-century visitor found additional evidence that prostitution was a healthy trade:

> [The prostitutes'] apartments are elegantly, and sometimes magnificently furnished; they keep several servants, and some have their own carriages. Many of them have annuities paid them by their seducers, and others settlements into which they have surprised their lovers at moments of intoxication. The testimony of these women, even of the lowest of them, is always received as evidence in the courts of justice. All this generally gives them a certain dignity of conduct, which can scarcely be reconciled with their profession.[4]

Moreover, though the trade of prostitution was certainly risky, large sums of money were occasionally made: Mrs. Hayes, who ran a society brothel, is said to have been worth twenty thousand pounds when she retired.[5]

Nonetheless, despite evidence that prostitution sometimes bore the mark of respectability, an equally powerful contemporaneous narrative insisted upon the insidious predatory nature of the procurer, who was almost always depicted as an older woman. Marcellus Laroon had memorialized the infamous Madam Creswell among his plates for *The Cryes of the City of London Drawne After Life* in 1687.[6] In the eighteenth-century the bawd who appears in the first plate of Hogarth's series *The Harlot's Progress* provided the prototype. Writer after writer seems to recall the scene depicted in this plate.[7]

"Madame Creswell." *From* Criers and Hawkers of London *by Marcellus Loon, Lilly Library, Indiana University, Bloomington, Indiana*

Plate 1 from *The Harlot's Progress* by Wiliam Hogarth. *Courtesy of the print collection of the Lewis Walpole Library, Yale University*

According to the OED, though the term *bawd* originally applied to men or women, after 1700 its use was "only feminine."[8] The word *pimp,* in contrast, rarely comes up in eighteenth-century discussions of prostitution. Similarly, prostitution is almost never discussed as men's work, even though men were certainly involved both as procurers and sex trade workers. The bawd, then, seems to have held a particular social fascination. Her presence allowed the popular imagination to isolate and fix on one source for the evils of prostitution. Stereotypic renderings the bawd's perfidy facilitated the notion that prostitution might be "rooted out" were it not for the perverse practices of these old women who mercilessly exploited ignorant young girls.[9]

If we return to Richardson, what the reader thinks about when confronted with Mrs. Sinclair is a behavior that is, paradoxically, so unnatural that only natural images can convey it. Animal imagery—hog, ferret, horse, perhaps the whale—suggest Mrs. Sinclair's aberration, her distance from a natural femininity. While pig parts (the bristles, the shortened nose) place her within the traditional grotesque, the dragon imagery gives her a mythical power.[10] But what is the source of Mrs. Sinclair's aberration? What makes her so "unnatural"? Perhaps, in the tradition that considered the prostitute herself, because of her overinvolvement with sex, something of a freak, she displays the moral dissolution thought to result from traffic in the sex trade.

But there is another possibility here as well. Seen against the discursive process we have identified, we recognize that Mrs. Sinclair embodies all the attributes to be eliminated by the new mercantilism. Her body—massive, sloppy, threatening—is what business discourse seeks to banish. Where texts like *The Mercantile Academy* proselytize for discipline and self-regulation, Mrs. Sinclair rages out of control. Where such texts urge constraints on speech, Mrs. Sinclair bellows noisily. Where the ideal is a homosocial community of men in business, Mrs. Sinclair is the grotesque female in business. Richardson makes her, in contrast to Postlethwayt's phoenixlike merchants, brutally mortal, not just animalistic but horrifying. On her death bed, she raves, howls, "more like a wolf than a human creature" (1387).

During the protracted illness that brings her death, Richardson draws the reader's attention away from Mrs. Sinclair to the prostitutes who have worked for her. Belford, writing to Lovelace, describes how daylight reveals the ravages of their work. The prostitutes have "faces, three or four of them, that had run, the paint lying in streaky seams not half blowzed off, discovering coarse wrinkled skins." Their unkempt hair similarly reveals how their glamorous nighttime appearance depends upon subterfuge and disguise: "The hair of some of them divers colours; obliged to the blacklead comb where black was affected; the artificial jet, however, yielding apace to the natural brindle: that of others plaistered with oil and powder, the oil predominating; but every one's hanging about her ears and neck in broken curls, or ragged ends" (1387). This bedraggled appearance, the result of the prostitutes being unprepared for Belford's gaze, is designed to unveil the prostitute's alluring surface, to warn the reader of the truth of the prostitute's body.

The modern reader might well find pathos in the image of these women, "unpadded, shoulder-bent, pallid-lipped, feeble-jointed wretches," who appear "from a blooming nineteen or twenty perhaps overnight, haggard well-worn strumpets of thirty-eight or forty." Perhaps our sympathy leads us to ask about the conditions of a life that takes this kind of toll. But their pathetic condition only unleashes an invective from Belford:

> I am the more particular in describing to thee the appearance these creatures made in my eyes when I came into the room, because I

believe thou never sawest any of them, much less a group of them, thus
unprepared for being seen. I, for my part, never did before; nor had I
now but upon this occasion been thus *favoured*. If thou *hadst*, I believe
thou wouldst hate a profligate woman as one of Swift's Yahoos or Vir-
gil's obscene Harpies squirting their ordure upon the Trojan trenchers;
since persons of such in their retirements are as filthy as their minds.
(1388)

The misogyny here is so obvious it almost warrants no comment. Belford
scapegoats the prostitute, making her body carry the weight for a deep cultural ambivalence about sexuality. The "filth" he finds in their bodies and
minds is a social product, for the whore is no more corrupt than the customer who visits her or the society that generates her presence.

Clearly Richardson borrows from Swift. The passage alludes to both "A
Beautiful Young Nymph Going to Bed" and book 4 of *Gulliver's Travels*, thereby
implicating Richardson in the same misogyny that has already been identified in Swift.[11] But the reference to Vergil is also powerful. In the *Aeneid* the
passage reads, "With virgin-faces, but with wombs obscene, / Foul paunches
and with ordure still unclean: / With claws for hands and looks for ever lean"
(1525n).[12] The opposition between the virgin face and the obscene womb
(perhaps a reference to the unnaturalness of the prostitute's sexual activity,
tied to her putative inability to procreate) reiterates a series of binary pairs
often linked to the prostitute's body: appearance versus reality, surface versus depth, outside versus inside. The last binary in particular has special res-
onance in antiprostitution discourse.

For Belford the world is neatly divided between two kinds of women. If
Lovelace could only have seen what he saw, he writes, he surely would "hate
[whores] as much as I do; and as much as I admire and next to adore a truly
virtuous and elegant woman; for to me it is evident that as a neat and clean
woman must be an angel of a creature, so a sluttish one is the impurest animal in nature" (1388). Thus the binaries continue: immoral versus virtuous,
filthy versus clean. Underlying these binaries is a basic opposition, selling
versus not selling, for, in the end, what distinguishes the virtuous woman
from the slut, what creates the crisis between appearance and reality, inside
and outside, is the fact that the prostitute sells her sexuality.

Though Belford's discussion is framed as moral polemic (and indeed its
ostensible purpose is to convince Lovelace of the error of his ways), what

really takes place here is the different placement of women within a system of exchange. As Catherine Gallagher explains, "In normal kinship arrangements, when the exchange is completed and the woman becomes a wife, she enters the realm of the "natural" (in the Aristotelian sense) production. But the prostitute never makes this transition from exchange to production; she retains her commodity form at all times."[13] Belford's prostitutes are, then, contaminated by their status as commodity. As women, they are filthy by virtue of the fact that they are wrongly placed within the business of society.

For Mary Douglas what is "dirty" offends against social order; the attempt to avoid "dirt" is an attempt to "make unity of experience." That is, attempts to purify serve "to impose system on an inherently untidy experience." She writes, "It is only by exaggerating the difference between within and without, above and below, male and female, with and against, that a semblance of order is created."[14] We can add clean/virtuous, filthy/corrupt to Douglas's list. But we also need to ask, *What* is being organized by means of this process? On the one hand, a patriarchal system of exchange is facilitated by the placing of female sexuality into categories. On the other hand, projective fears about the nature of *human* sexuality itself are handled by means of this division of sexual behavior into two components—a "legitimate" expression, to take place only with the confines of marriage, and a persistently "illegitimate" component, which (as some eighteenth-century writers argue) must be dealt with somehow.

Because prostitution is an event that allows for displacement and projection, mid-eighteenth-century discussions of its existence rarely address the thing itself. That is, female prostitution is hardly ever explicitly discussed as women's *work*. Missing from this discussion is the perspective of someone involved in the profession. The prostitute is imagined along the lines of the jolly hooker, as in the *Nocturnal Revels*, or as the putrefying whore, as in *Clarissa*, but she is never seen as a woman who labors.[15] What were the conditions of the sex trade? How did actual prostitutes understand their lot?

And yet paradoxically, despite this cultural gap, polemics about prostitution in mid-eighteenth-century Britain implicitly broach the topic of business more often than sex or morality. Two questions arise repeatedly in discussions about prostitution: first, "What kind of place is a house of prostitution?" or, more broadly, "What is the proper space for business?" Second, "What ought to be the nature of business?" or, more precisely, "What is the nature of *men's* business?" Though prostitution is said to be the oldest profession in the world, and though its existence in mid-century Britain was scarcely new, an intensified emphasis on the "reform" of prostitutes appeared in the early decades of the eighteenth century.[16] Thus reformist texts— without specifically referring to prostitution as women's *work*—participated in the cultural project of defining women's *business*.

As we have previously seen, over the course of the eighteenth century retail space was gradually codified. Selling, which once took place outdoors, happened more and more often indoors. This movement was both literal and metaphorical, as interior space generated interiorized practices of salesmanship. In addition, the movement was toward isolating retail space and removing it from the family setting. The salesman was to separate his passions from his business manners as clearly as he was to separate his family from his customers. By the end of the century wealthier tradesmen no longer lived above their shops, thereby ensuring the total separation of the place of business from the home. This evolution in retail practice was consistent with the larger cultural trend to see business and domestic life as discrete spheres of activity.

In the case of prostitution, however, selling occurred in a space that defied boundaries. If house and shop were to be discrete locations, the whorehouse was a house that conducted itself as a shop. It offered for public sale what ought to have been a private affair, conflating the space of business with the space of domesticity. It greatly disturbed the reformer Saunders Welch, for example, to see "women publickly exposing themselves at windows and doors of bawdy-houses like beasts in a market for public sale, with language, dress, and gesture too offensive to mention." His aim was to stop "open and publick traffick of bawds in houses solely appropriate to that purpose, by exposing women at their windows and doors, as tradesmen do their goods for sale."[17] If he hated the sight of prostitutes publicly advertising themselves, making houses into places of sale, it disturbed him even more when houses of prostitution passed for ordinary houses, when houses of ill-repute were indistinguishable from respectable domiciles. Indeed, contemporaneous foreign travelers such as D'Archenholz commented upon the ready accessibility of prostitution under the most innocent guises. He claims that even married women were known to come to Westminster, where they would be unknown for short periods of time, after which time they would return home.[18]

Richardson, of course, capitalizes upon this indistinguishableness in *Clarissa*. Lovelace is able to bring Clarissa into a whorehouse precisely because Mrs. Sinclair does not advertise her business. A rental agent describes the layout of Mrs. Sinclair's property:

> She rents two good houses, distant from each other, only joined by a large handsome passage. The inner house is the genteelest, and is very elegantly furnished; but you may have the use of a very handsome parlor in the outer house, if you choose to look into the street.
>
> A little garden belongs to the inner house, in which the old gentlewoman has displayed a true female fancy, and crammed it with vases, flower pots and figures without number. . . . The apartments she has to let are in the inner house: they are a dining-room, two neat parlours, a withdrawing-room, two or three handsome bedchambers (one with a pretty light closet in it, which looks out into the little garden); all furnished in taste. (470)

The more Clarissa finds evidence of Mrs. Sinclair's gentility in her taste, her knickknacks, and her flowers, the more horrifying is the scene; for the semblance of respectability functions as a stage set, a backdrop against which many illicit acts would have occurred. Yet despite the nature of Mrs. Sinclair's house, Clarissa is unable to distinguish it from any other. To her eye, nothing in its appearance betrays the purpose of the layout or the rooms. Similarly, the women who work for Mrs. Sinclair, though somewhat suspicious in their demeanor, are not readily identified as prostitutes by Clarissa.

Richardson would have us believe (in keeping with contemporaneous accounts) that the business of prostitution was sometimes indistinguishable from everyday domesticity. Yet this is precisely what is supposed to shock his reader the most: if vice can look so respectable, how is one to avoid it? What distinguishes legitimate domestic practice from a rampant sexual underworld? What recourse can one take in a world where what passes for domestic life is actually a front for the merchandising of sex? Thus the business of prostitution proves most offensive when it imitates the semblance of everyday life. In *Clarissa*, then, Richardson must also punish Mrs. Sinclair for her encroachments upon the domestic. Her histrionic death satisfies the reader's impulse to purge the domestic of what so seriously compromises it.

When the business of prostitution presents itself so innocently, thriving in the very heart of the metropolis, how do reformers respond? In *A Proposal to Render Effectual a Plan to Remove the Nuisance of Common Prostitutes from the*

Streets of this Metropolis, Saunders Welch expresses his concern with the twenty-fifth statute under George II, which allowed justices of the peace to prosecute anyone identified as plying the sex trade in a written oath by "two inhabitants of the parish paying scot and lot" and who entered into "a recognizance of twenty pounds each to procure evidence." What is interesting about Welch's proposal is how it testifies to contemporaneous difficulty with prosecuting offenders when those offenders were passing as respectable citizens. The statute seems to have been an attempt to root out sex businesses that had thoroughly infiltrated everyday life. Lamenting public reluctance to inform on one's neighbors, Saunders proposes an alternative solution: transport the keepers of bawdy houses and create a hospital where prostitutes might be confined and reformed.

Like other disciplinary sites, Welch's proposed hospital is a space for regularizing and controlling the body, for confronting an apparently resistant sexuality and for rendering it docile, compliant both outside and inside. He hopes that penitent prostitutes would "voluntarily offer themselves" (26) to his hospital. While there, the women would wear uniforms and participate in a work program. The most chilling part of Welch's proposal is his means for ensuring the prostitute's total compliance. If, for example, she "swears, curses, or acts indecently" while in the hospital, the governors should "order her reasonable corporal punishment immediately" or "mulct [*sic*] her in her needs until the next meeting and also place some badge or mark of ignominy on her for a week" (28). The hospital itself must be divided into two parts, one part for the truly penitent, and the other "for those apprehended in their crimes, who though they excite commiseration as distressed fellow creatures, ought to be dealt with in a different manner, so as to render their confinement in the eyes of the vulgar a kind of punishment" (39). He elaborates, "This would prevent some from deviating from virtue, and induce the penitent who might be sincerely desirous to present herself to be received into the hospital as a place of retreat from contempt and misery, and thereby avoid the shame of being apprehended and exposed in a court of justice, and abiding it's [*sic*] sentence" (39). Welch's logic here seems ambivalent: the hospital is both a retreat and a punishment. It is both an alternative to the shame of arrest and a place where one might be shamed into submission.

The impulse behind this text is the containment, isolation, and control of the prostitute's "nature."[19] Yet Welch's constant reference to the fate of unreformed prostitutes or "repeat offenders"—transportation—suggests that he knows containment is not necessarily the solution. Like the bawds who are presumably beyond hope from the very beginning, the unreformed prostitute must be removed from society. However, Welch never acknowledges the conditions that lead a woman to become a prostitute or that compel her to return to her trade. He imagines reformed prostitutes being reclaimed by "parents, friends, or a housekeeper" (41). But how many women would have had such a place to go? The respectable domesticity that Welch so desires requires a basic standard of living. As Mary Wollstonecraft wrote, "Asylums and Magdalens are not the proper remedies for [the abuses of prostitution]. It is justice, not charity, that is wanting in the world."[20]

Unlike Welch, other reformers more readily acknowledge that adverse economic circumstances may have driven women into prostitution. In 1758, for example, John Fielding writes, "I have before observed that the Trades for employing women are too few, and that those which women might execute are engrossed by Men, and that many Women have not the Opportunity of learning even those which Women do follow, on account of the Premiums paid for learning the said Business." His solution is to provide training for "fallen women" in such traditional women's trades such as mantua making, stay making, and child's coat making.[21] Similarly, Jonas Hanway envisioned a carpet manufactory as the solution to women's employment problems. However, for Hanway, as for other reformers, the issue of the prostitute's rehabilitation remained the pressing concern. Hanway was convinced that after a period of probation, hard-working women would "wipe off the stains" of their former situation and would be married by "some rare geniuses" who would appreciate their wives' ability to support themselves.[22] This ongoing concern with the reformed prostitute's reintegration into society is yet another aspect of a social obsession with containing prostitution, for in arguing that the prostitute's stains can be removed, Hanway implicitly argues that she exists in a problematic relationship to her society.[23]

In contrast to Welch, Mandeville is cheerfully ready to acknowledge that prostitutes cannot be reformed. In *A Modest Defense of Public Stews* he writes, "But the Minds of Women are observ'd to be so much corrupted by the Reproach they suffer upon that loss [of their virtuous reputation], that they seldom or never change that Course of Life [as prostitutes] for the better."[24] Convinced that "some women are naturally more chaste" or "less amorous than others" (42), Mandeville traces the propensity toward prostitution to the prostitute's body itself: "There are some Women who have the Nerves of their Pudenda more lively, and endow'd with a quicker Sensation than others" (42).[25] Because the prostitute's own body dictates her choice of a profession, Mandeville reasons that the best course of action is to regularize her existence in a state-run house of prostitution. Like Welch, Mandeville also wishes to contain prostitutes, but, rather than reforming them, he wishes to have their services readily available to men who cannot possibly, he argues, carry on their business without this sexual service. For him the issues are the nature of male sexuality and the constitution of a business that might best serve that nature.

Sex in Mandeville's treatise for both men and women is an essentialized impulse toward what one would rather not do but must anyhow. Like Lillo, he locates a biological imperative toward mating that disrupts the necessary course of business. Unlike Lillo, he argues that it is best to indulge it. For example, he laments, "But alas! the violent Love for Women is born and bred with us, nay, it is so absolutely necessary to our being born at all. And however people may pretend, that unlawful Enjoyment is contrary to the Laws of *Nature*; this is certain that Nature never fails to furnish us largely with this Passion" (6–7).

If the "violent love" for women is disruptive, what it particularly endangers is a man's ability to carry out his business:

> For let a Man have ever so much Business; it can't stop the Circulation
> of his Blood, or prevent the Seminal Secretion: for Sleeping, or Walk-
> ing the Spermaticks will do their Office, 'tho a Man's Thoughts may be
> so much employ'd about Other Affairs, that he cannot attend to every
> minute Titillation. A Man of Pleasure, indeed, may make his copulative
> Science his whole study; and by Idleness and Luxury, nay prompt
> Nature that way, and spur up the spirits of Wantonness. (22–23)

While repression may offer temporary respite from the struggle, businessmen's "abstinence contributes to heighten the Violence of the Desire and to make it more irresistible" (24).

That Mandeville's version of male sexuality is both essentialist and heterosexist is obvious. But notice also the social assumptions about business that are enabled by this view. First Mandeville introduces the notion that the smooth functioning of "business as usual" depends upon the sexual availability of some women whose nature it is to perform that service. As Laura Mandell writes, Mandeville "animates the evils to be excluded from the ideal of prudent business management in the figure of the prostitute."[26] Second, he contributes to the cultural construction of business as a distinctly masculine act that can only occur if male sexuality has been indulged. He gives license to male sexual indulgence as the cornerstone of "good business."

If we return to the discursive context in which Mandeville's argument appears, we see that, *even if this text is intended as satire*, it is consistent with several other historical trends. Once again, for example, it isolates the businessman's body from his mind, his passions from his intellect. The same body and the same passions that are recognized only to be "mastered" in the writings of Defoe, Postlethwayt, or Lillo are here indulged. And women are called upon to make the body their business. This occurs at the same historical moment when other kinds of employment opportunities are being disallowed to women. Or, as we have seen, it happens simultaneously with the perception that women in legitimate businesses are actually in the business of the body, as was the case with milliners and mantua makers who were assumed to be sexually available.

We could also think about the representation of male sexuality in Mandeville's text in another way: here male sexuality—imagined in both essentialist and heterosexist terms—is represented as alien to men themselves, that is, as a wanton, irrepressible force that rises up and thwarts their best efforts to be men doing the business of men. Male sexuality, residing within the male body itself, is undisciplined and subversive. It is, metaphorically speaking, the feminine part of the male body. The prostitute's body reflects back to the male subject the image of his own undisciplined sexual impulses. In looking at her, he sees what he either abhors or indulges in himself. The effort to reform or regulate prostitution is, then, the effort to take control of what is imagined as feminine within a male cultural project.[27] Mandeville differs from reformers who would isolate, imprison, or expel a feminine sexuality in only his strategy. Rather than repressing feminine sexuality, his project is to master it by indulging it in a regulated way.

To conclude, in the effort toward the discursive construction of business as both male and masculine, prostitution is problematic because it keeps both women and the feminine in business. Historically speaking, sex has sometimes become women's work when few alternatives have existed. We have seen that a young woman in the late eighteenth century, considering the possibility of economic self-sufficiency through business, would have faced several obstacles. First, her legal status as feme covert was matched by the social projection of her weakness, irresponsibility, and need for constant supervision. Competing accounts of the respectability of women's businesses would have sent a mixed message at best, until public opinion had shifted to equate women's businesses with prostitution. That is, by the end of the century public opinion appears to have fixed on the notion that women's business was the business of the body. A woman either entered into marriage, thereby giving up her body to childbearing and nurturing, or she used her body to serve the needs of men outside of marriage. Yet the negative ideological shift away from the notion of legitimate women's businesses occurred in a setting where many women certainly needed to work. Women obviously continued to circumnavigate the narrow social definition of women's business, finding useful employment in the process. Historical evidence also suggests that many women did the "business of the body."

The conflation of women with "the feminine" in business and the removal of the feminine from business had reverberations we still feel today. Women in late twentieth-century America feel compelled by a shifting capitalist economy as never before to return to business, yet many report feeling unwelcome in a male business environment. While their experiences range from merely uncomfortable to hostile, they soon encounter what is now identified as the glass ceiling. And popular media are scarcely sympathetic to their plight: in movies like *Disclosure* Mrs. Sinclair has been transformed into Demi Moore. Though Demi Moore's nearly mythical physique (so slim, so toned after all those children!) is antithetical to Mrs. Sinclair's corpulence, it performs a similar function. It too is a negative site of projection; it also fixates attention on what should never make its way into business. Reduced to her body, Moore's persona in *Disclosure* depicts a feminine wantonness and irregularity that men *must*—but somehow *cannot*—stay clear of. Similarly, in the contemporary business setting well-disciplined, muscled female flesh can be just as threatening—and powerful—as corporeal grossness.[28] Indications of female self-control have paradoxically become as disturbing as "too much" female flesh. *Disclosure* conflates irregular business practice with the irregularities inherent in female sexuality, and it serves the status quo by vilifying the feminine in business and by insisting upon its expulsion.

In conclusion, a feminist critique of business could do one of several things. First, it could argue for the inclusion of women in a business environment; it could point to the historical patterns of isolation and discrimination that have led to an unnatural distribution of labor, and it could seek to redress those inequities. Simultaneously, it could argue that business needs to become more accommodating to women's lives, that it must make space for family issues and concerns, allow time for family needs in general and for mothers' needs in particular. But this politics of inclusion, while it puts women back in business, may not go far enough. A more militant feminist critique would, perhaps, focus upon the discursive processes that have aligned the feminine with "not-business." Recognizing that the feminine has been culturally encoded with a series of qualities—physicality, wantonness, irregularity—we could argue that these qualities are neither essentially female nor necessarily antithetical to good business. We might insist, in other words, on the redefinition of good business itself in such a way that allows for passion, for irregularity, even occasional wantonness, when those characteristics serve human needs. A feminist critique could point out the mistakes of trying to expel the feminine from business or the equally grave dangers of seeking to manipulate it.[29] That critique could work with the paradoxical formulation we have seen so far, tapping into a power that seems most resistant at the moment of its apparent mastery and making it the means of cultural change.

Conclusion

> I want a car, I want to be with the man I love, I want a nice home, away
> from New York, up the Peekskills, or maybe in Florida, or somewhere
> far, where no one knows me. . . . I want my sex change. . . . I want to get
> married in church in white. . . . I want to be a complete woman. . . . And
> I want to be a professional model, behind cameras, in the high fashion
> world. . . . I *want* this. This is what I want. And I'm going to go for it.

This is the personal testimony of a transsexual named Venus Xtravaganza in
the documentary film *Paris is Burning* (1992).[1] It is as mundane as it is contradictory. The least enfranchised member of society yearns for domestic
stability, for all the trappings of bourgeois respectability. Making her living
on the streets of Harlem, Venus is far from the Peekskills. Her dream of marriage extenuates the symbolism of the traditional patriarchal wedding. The
white dress adorning the transsexual body critiques the notion of the vir-
ginal body. Even her name undermines male traffic in women: *Xtravaganza*
marks not her patrimony but her self-chosen place in a familylike affiliation
of gay and transsexual men with a similar sensibility.

Venus Xtravaganza exposes contradictions that belong to culture at large
as well as herself. She wants simultaneously to be protected by domesticity,
unknown by anyone, and exposed by celebrity, known by everyone. She mis-
speaks the preposition *behind* to explain her fantasy of fame—"behind cam-

eras in the high fashion world"—but this slip suggests the profound ambivalence in the dream: she wants to be in control of a situation she construes to be controlling her. Venus wants no more than what generations of American girls were once told to want—financial security through marriage to a man with a good income. And she is utterly clear about the price of that security. When pressed to clarify whether she herself trades sex for money, she reasons, "But I feel like, if you're married, a woman, in the suburbs, a regular woman, married to her husband, and she wants him to buy her a washer and dryer set, I'm sure she'd have to go to bed with him anyway to give him what he wants in order to get what she wants."

It is not surprising that Venus alludes to marriage as legalized prostitution. But her phrase "regular woman" is powerfully resonant, for Venus adheres to the notion that an inextricable connection exists between essentialized femininity, the world of commodities, and a patriarchal economy. To that extent, she has internalized well the themes of this study. "I want to be a complete woman," she insists, "I want my sex change." She cannot imagine achieving financial security in her current body. For her, being a "complete woman" depends upon having the biological features of a woman. However, a complete woman is also a privileged economic category. A complete woman is someone who has successfully used her body to traffic for financial security, for a world of coveted commodities and "luxury." Venus has learned that the business of a complete woman who wants a place within a patriarchal economy is to make her body available to others. But she is never able to capitalize on her insight: by the end of the film we learn of her brutal murder, presumably at the hands of one of her clients.

I could argue that the cultural history I have been tracing, which starts with the consumer revolution in eighteenth-century England, culminates with the story of Venus Xtravaganza in late twentieth-century America. For this history has been the story of how Anglo-American culture constructed female subjectivity in relation to the emerging practices of consumerism. Onto the category of "woman" that culture simultaneously projected its deepest anxieties about and its greatest hopes for powerful acts of consumption. In its earliest phases, the "consumer revolution" fixated on the female body as a disciplinary site. Working along class lines, advocates for consumerism placed some women at the tea table, subjecting them to its regularizing and normalizing rituals. Other women, laboring women in particular, could be enjoined similarly to consume, but only after their appetites had been managed. Rapidly expanding consumer practices in the West occurred against a backdrop of colonial expansion, bringing the British consumer into contact with her dark sister, the underimagined female Caribbean slave, whose labors would help fuel the British economy.

Also during the eighteenth century the discursive construction of business as male and masculine—and ultimately as *white* and Anglo-Saxon—was enforced by a cultural understanding of women's business as the body. Having been denied access to legitimate opportunities to do business, women were called upon to do the business of the body—either as childbearing nurturers or as prostitutes who served the carnal needs of the business community.[2] This certainly did not mean that women ceased to work, but it did mean that women's work could only be understood or evaluated from the viewpoint of a patriarchal economy. In a misogynist climate, whatever a woman's actual employment, her culturally decreed mission is the work of the body.

In twentieth-century America Venus Xtravaganza was born biologically male but economically disadvantaged and racially other in a society that fails to make business opportunities available to the disenfranchised.[3] Like the gay men in the film, Venus can only fantasize about access to economic power. And because she fails to identify with a male ethos, she taps into the cultural fantasy that is the legacy of the process we have been studying, namely, the dream of becoming a biological female who somehow makes her body the site of a successful business endeavor. Her violent death comments on the tragic inadequacy of this means.

Yet why does Venus insist on a connection between the *female* body and commodities? The consumer revolution of the eighteenth-century only brought into sharper relief a preexisting, profound social ambivalence about consumption. Economic consumption—the recourse to goods and services designed to make life easier, more commodious, "better"—has been historically metaphorized as a bodily process. Consumption is about appetite, about tastes that are both literal and metaphorical. It is also about addiction, and the first experiences of many modern consumers began with products that were quite literally addictive—coffee, tea, and tobacco. The early discourses of consumption were grounded in an understanding of bodily need and compulsion. In truth, consumption far surpasses the body; even in the eighteenth century it rapidly became a function of projection, fantasy, and desire more than bodily need. Nonetheless, today metaphors of the body still anchor public discussion of consumer trends.[4] The understanding of consumption as a bodily phenomenon in turn facilitated the language of retail trade. The customer found herself poised *as a body* on the verge of seduction or mastery; she was urged to yield herself up, or let herself be taken over by the luxuries of the marketplace.

Yet a patriarchal ideology has a lot at stake in preserving the notion that women are the body, that they are closer to the physical, and that, unlike men, they are unable to easily resist the dictates of the body. In the shift to industrial capitalism this perception of women as the body was crucial to the creation of what is commonly called the separate spheres. The world of business, enterprise, and commerce became the world of men. It also became the world that supposedly transcended the body. In the meantime, the domestic world, the center of family, childbearing, and child rearing, was constructed as the world of women and the body. Indeed, home was construed as the legitimate place to do "the business of the body." Sex outside of marriage, pregnancy out of wedlock, were problematic because they indicated that an action had been performed out of context.

Because women were, according to tradition, aligned with the body and because consumption itself was already understood as a bodily phenomenon, women became the full target for the intensified discourses of consumerism. Because they were perceived as being eternally labile, involved in physical processes like birth and nurturing, barely eluding the mysterious dictates of their own bodies, women were assumed to be "natural" consumers. Their passions, ever ready to be tapped, their innumerable desires, rooted in an domineering physiology, drove them to buy with alarming rapidity, with reckless disregard for cost (or so common wisdom held). These cliched notions of an essential femininity were reinforced by an economic reality: beginning in the late eighteenth century women were placed in the marketplace as the primary purchasers for all commodities relating to domestic life. It was their decreed purpose to spend money in order to make life comfortable for others. The fact that not all women had the resources to consume did not exempt them from this ideological onslaught. The dream of an essentialized feminine power to consume was held out to all women, regardless of class or race or economic circumstance. As we have seen, this is the dream that shapes Venus's life. Thus the eighteenth century saw only the inception of a consumer discourse that encompassed the definition of female subjectivity, and we might pause to suggest quickly the history of women and consumption that ensues. We follow an arc that will take us from the eighteenth-century British tea table to the marketing of a doll in twentieth-century America.

Many cultural historians identify the department store as the crucial setting for the creation of the modern female consumer, or "the new woman."[5] The founding of the Bon Marché in Paris in 1852 was followed by the Magazin du Louvre in 1855 and Printemps in 1865. In the United States Marshall Fields, Macy's, and Wanamakers were all established by the 1880s. Critics like Remy Saisselin celebrate the architectural triumph of these new public spaces, finding in their histories the story of female "liberation": with the implementation of *entrée libre,* women found themselves able to wander freely through spectacular displays of goods from all over the globe. For Saisselin, department stores offered women unprecedented educational opportunities: "stores evolved from mere merchandising novelties into centers where one might learn interior decoration; later they turned into restaurants, even art galleries, educating the palate as well as the eye." Indeed, he insists on the similarity between the museum and the department store: "Although the differences between art and commerce, objet d'art and consumer objects, were stressed on the social, aesthetic, and theoretical level, the similarities, among the structures, space, and methods of exhibiting objects in museums and departments store remained striking."[6]

However, not all cultural historians share Saisselin's enthusiasm for the department store. Rachel Bowlby, deploying the work of Baudrillard, queries the nature of the relationship between the consumer and the objects so alluringly displayed:

> The consumer is not (just) an active appropriator of objects for sale.
> His or her identity, the constitution of the self as a social subject, a "citizen of consumer society," depends on the acquisition of appropriate
> objects. . . . There is thus a clear sense in which the consumer citizen
> is not so much possessor of as possessed by the commodities which one
> must have to be made or to make oneself in the form objectively guaranteed as that of a social individual.[7]

Thus, before subscribing to the notion of the department store as the site of women's empowerment, Bowlby would further examine the dynamics of commodity exchange: what power does any consumer—and the female consumer in particular—hold? And, despite his fondness for the department store, even Saisselin writes of the confusion of the female consumer and the object she would consume: "Woman herself turns into a most expensive bibelot and yet is, at the same time, a voracious consumer of luxury and accumulator of bibelots."[8]

Like Bowlby and Saisselin, Anne Friedberg emphasizes how the revolution in retail trade resulted in important changes in physical spaces like arcades and department stores. Friedberg's interest lies with an increased consumer mobility and with what she defines as a "virtual gaze": "not a direct perception but a received *perception* mediated through representation."[9] Friedberg argues that the nineteenth century saw the creation of a *flaneuse,* a female version of the *flaneur.* Her concept of the flaneuse embraces both the notion of the department store as site of new freedoms and the feminist critique of women and commodification.[10] For Friedberg accessible public retail space is linked in important ways to other public spaces where the gaze is directed in meaningful ways; the cinema becomes a logical extension of the shopper's experience. Friedberg brings us up to the contemporary scene: "The shopping mall appears to be a historical endpoint of increasing female empowerment, a 'Ladies' Paradise' for the contemporary flaneuse." Yet Friedberg also reminds us of the complicated interplay between "looking" and "buying" and she suggests that many modern female consumers enact a "vicarious" economic empowerment: because of the ready accessibility of credit cards, "instead of deferring payment to a husband or father, [today's female consumer] defers payment to the bank."[11]

Several themes unite these discussions. First, all three writers concur that retail spaces like the department store—and, still later, the mall—had important ramifications for the definition of modern female subjectivity. For all the physical space of retail activity is an important psychological space as well, one that is antithetical to the insularity of home and potentially oppositional to conservative domestic ideology. These cultural historians offer us a range of opinions concerning the nature of female consumer activity. Shopping is both the expression of active agency and the sign that the shopper has internalized powerfully coercive messages. The shopper makes her choices; she purposefully and intelligently finds her way through the maze of goods. But, in some sense, the shopper's choices have already been made for her; her agency is only an illusion in a culture where commodities tell us who we are.[12]

Running parallel to the ongoing debate about whether female consumerism can be a form of empowerment is the discussion of what it means
for women to be identified as a "market." For many late twentieth-century
feminists Betty Friedan's *Feminist Mystique* was a formative text. Friedan
identified the thwarted dreams, repressed ambition, and manifest discon-
tent of the middle-class American housewife and she traced the source of
female unhappiness to an oppressive image of femininity. She located this
image in women's magazines, Freud, social scientists like Margaret Mead,
and, above all, Madison Avenue. Madison Avenue had created the "true
housewife," the paradigmatic female consumer, who knuckled under to the
will of male advertisers. As Mica Nava writes, Friedan—like Herbert Mar-
cuse—"operated with the conviction that cultural forms have the power to
construct 'false needs,' to indoctrinate and manipulate men and women into
social conformity and subordination."[13] The solution, Friedan suggested,
was "to just say no":

> Once a woman stops trying to make cooking, cleaning, washing, iron-
> ing, "something more," she can say "no, I don't want a stove with
> rounded corners, I don't want four different kinds of soap." She can say
> "no" to those mass daydreams of the women's magazines and televi-
> sion, "no" to the depth researchers and manipulators who are trying to
> run her life. Then, she can use the vacuum cleaner and the dishwasher
> and all the automatic appliances, and even the instant mashed potatoes
> for what they are truly worth—to save time that can be used in more
> creative ways.[14]

Writing thirty years later in a book entitled *Where the Girls Are: Growing Up
Female with the Mass Media,* Susan Douglas updates *The Feminine Mystique.*
Douglas answers that it seems unlikely women ever simply said "yes" to the
images offered by advertisers. Women were most likely conflicted from the
start; the possibility of rebellion was always there. Even highly retrograde
television shows like *I Dream of Genie* offered one version of the subversive
potential of femininity. Where Friedan saw women as passively assimilating
an insidious sales pitch, Douglas argues that being identified as a "market"
was an equivocal event. Though the intent might have been to capture and
exploit a vulnerable audience, in the case of younger women a sense of
group identity unintentionally emerged:

So at the same time that the makers of Pixie bands, Maybelline eye-liner, Breck shampoo, and *Beach Blanket Bingo* reinforced our roles as cute, airheaded girls, the mass media produced a teen girl popular culture of songs, movies, TV shows, and magazines that cultivated in us a highly self-conscious sense of importance, difference, and even rebellion. Because young women became critically important economically, as a market, the suspicion began to percolate among them, over time, that they might be important culturally, and then politically, as a generation. Instead of co-opting rebellion, the media actually helped to promote it.[15]

However, the relationship between the media and a consumer group identified as a market is never static. Corporate America once again took the upper hand, interpreting the goals of women's liberation as a form of female narcissism. As Douglas explains:

> Women's liberation became equated with women's ability to do whatever they wanted for themselves, whenever they wanted, no matter what the expense. . . . There was an enormous emphasis on luxury, and on separating oneself from the less enlightened, less privileged herd. The ability to spend time and money on one's appearance was a sign of personal success and of breaking away from the old roles and rules that held women down in the past. Break free from those old conventions, the ads urged, and get *truly* liberated: put yourself first.[16]

In other words, by insisting that feminism was narcissism, corporate America accomplished several ends: it mitigated the collective ideals of early feminism and redirected "sisterhood" back toward competition. Furthermore, it trivialized the philosophical and ethical bases upon which feminism was built. While feminism promoted self-discovery and individual development, it never suggested that you "put yourself first." Finally, this corporate strategy reintroduced the body as the organizing principle of female subjectivity. By depicting the female body in relation to self-indulgence, advertisers once again moved women further along the axis that runs from commodity to luxury. To be positioned in this way is to be denied one's status as a useful contributing member of society. We come away from Douglas's book with the message that it is not enough to resist; we must constantly remain informed and alert. While it never hurts to look good, "looking good" is not always a matter of spending lots of money on one's body. Feminism in particular can provide us with a useful set of tools for understanding our place within consumer culture.

Thus the history of consumer culture in general, and the history of women and consumer culture in particular, is multivalent; it tells us several truths at once. First, consumerism is most powerful when it appears to be about choices. Indeed, its very appeal, as Judith Williamson writes, may lie in the promise it always tenders of a kind of agency. Ultimately, the "choice" has already been made for us, and yet it would be a mistake to underestimate the psychic power that inheres in the notion of choice. Second, there is nothing that cannot be appropriated by consumer discourse, but this does not mean that people are passive dupes. Sometimes we are vulnerable; at other times we are resilient, resourceful at finding a sense of community, or even solidarity, where it is not supposed to be found.

Nowhere is the multivalence of consumer discourse more apparent, perhaps, than in the marketing of what we sell our children. In conclusion, then, I offer one especially rich example of the intersection of late twentieth-century consumerism and female subjectivity—the American Girls doll collection. These dolls are offered by the Pleasant Company as an alternative to the mass-produced—and much maligned—fantasies of femininity in the form of Polly Pockets, Strawberry Shortcake, and, of course, Barbie dolls. Sold exclusively by mail-order catalog, the American Girls collection consists of five dolls, each tied to a historical period. The dolls are named Felicity ("1774: A spunky, spritely colonial girl"), Kirsten ("1854: A pioneer girl of strength and spirit), Addy ("1864: A courageous girl of the Civil War"), Samantha ("1904: A bright Victorian beauty"), and Molly ("1944: a lively, lovable schemer and dreamer") Though all the dolls are "American girls," all are white, except Addy, who is African American. None of the dolls (so far) is Jewish; none is Asian.[17] None is designed to be even remotely of interest to a boy (though surely some boys *are* interested in them). Each comes with an extensive—and very expensive—set of clothes and accessories, all of which are beautifully manufactured. Samantha's "complete collection," consisting of doll, clothing, doll furniture, and accessories, will set the indulgent parent or grandparent back $995.

The catalog also markets six books for each doll, six books in which the doll character is featured. The books are also well produced, on good paper with skillful illustrations; the stories are well written. As though influenced by New Historicism, each tries faithfully to convey something about race, class, or gender in the historical period. Each book culminates with "A Peek Into the Past," a short section with historical text, documentary photographs, and illustrations. In *Meet Samantha*, for example, the eight-year-old reader learns that "the lives of the servants were not very comfortable or elegant. Servants worked long days for little money. . . . Servants were expected to do this work without complaint and to keep their 'proper' place—separate from the family they worked for."[18] In *Meet Molly* she encounters images of Rosie the Riveter, a Victory Garden, and a "Blue Star Mother."

However, this admirable effort toward historic specificity is somewhat mitigated by the design of the series. Though the dolls are identified with different historical periods, and the series are written by different authors, each book series goes through exactly the same sequence—for each, the first book is entitled *Meet [Doll Name]*, the second *[Doll Name] Learns a Lesson*, the third *[Doll Name's] Surprise*, the fourth *Happy Birthday [Doll Name]*, the fifth *[Doll Name] Saves the Day*, and the sixth *Changes for [Doll Name]*. Thus, whether the doll character lives on the American prairie in the 1860s or in a midwestern suburb during World War II, she undergoes the same formative experiences. And those experiences are tied to the dolls' accessories, faithfully reproduced and available through the catalog.

This combination of historical specificity and universalized girlhood leads to some rather odd representations. Felicity, as an American colonial, is the closest to the eighteenth-century woman who has been the subject of this book. The catalog copy is attentive to the tea table as a central location of Felicity's learning, or "school story." It adds, however, a peculiarly American twist: "Learning the tea ceremony is fun until Felicity's father decides that the king's tax on tea is unfair, and he refuses to sell tea in his store or to drink it in the Merriman household. How can Felicity continue the tea lesson she loves and still be loyal to her father?"[19] Here both paternal and national loyalties are put forth as central themes in the life of a typical "American girl." In rewriting history so that it is accessible to the daughter of an affluent, twentieth-century American family, the copy also provides a normative version of girlhood in which the eight-year-old consumer is encouraged to see her life along a continuum of quintessentially female experience. The tea table, the copy seems to suggest, is the place where American girls first learned their lessons.

In order to play out Felicity's experience, the young consumer will want to possess the required accessories. Here is everything Felicity needs to practice the proper tea ceremony. The catalog copy describes the items:

Tea leaves were stored in a wooden *tea caddy*. Felicity's dark blue *teacup* and *saucer* have an elegant fruit pattern on them. There is no handle on the small china teacup, which came from China back then. Put the *spoon* on the saucer, her cotton *napkin* in her lap, and pass her a *queen cake*. Just be sure her loose tooth doesn't fall out when she takes a bite! How embarrassing! $22[20]

Thus, in this most innocent way, modern girls are introduced to the historical disciplining of the female body: *they* can practice the placement of a spoon, the delicate art of managing a plate. Once again, as before, physicality is a problem: the best effort at self-discipline can be thwarted by a body that goes through its transitions regardless of the setting. If this passage seems a bit banal, it is also freighted with historical memory. For now, as then, what a young consumer needs to learn is how successfully to guide her body through the wilderness of familial and social expectation.

In this way the American Girls dolls offer a version of history in which the past is different but also exactly the same. While the catalog outwardly celebrates female independence, agency, self-sufficiency, intelligence, it also insistently normalizes girlhood, collapsing the story of developing female subjectivity into predictable and "normal" patterns. The attempt at normalizing is least successful in the case of Addy, who, when her series begins, is not only "a courageous girl of the Civil War" but also a *slave*. Her story is arguably the most realistic in the group. For example, in *Meet Addy*, Addy is whipped by the master while she holds onto her father, as he is about to be sold to another plantation.[21]

While liberals parents (and I include myself here) certainly appreciate the effort to educate children about the horrors of slavery, it seems far-fetched to suggest that Addy's real milestones are the normal ones: is the story of her nascent citizenship really served by the six-book series? In the end the horrors of her beginning give way to "Church Fair Fun" (an accessory pack consisting of a puppet show and a slide whistle, $22) and "Addy's party treats" (imitation flowers, miniature milk bottle, pie plate, pie server, as well as a "patriotic *banner of freedom*" for $24).[22] Thus even slavery becomes a marketable condition, when it leads to the accumulation of the appropriate accessories.

What, then, do girls ultimately learn from playing with these dolls? What do parents get from buying them? And what does this example teach us about women and consumer culture? Certainly girls who are lucky enough to own these dolls and accessories receive, on some level, a positive image. The notion of historical identification with eight-year-old girls of the past cannot be lightly dismissed, and a sense of solidarity with generations of American girls (however those generations are constructed) is a positive achievement. From playing with these dolls, imaginatively living out their stories, young girls do participate in the reinsertion of women into American history. This reinsertion was, of course, a key goal of feminist scholars in the 1960s and the 1970s. But ultimately this fantasy of female agency is an imaginative act that has already been shaped for our daughters. We, their affluent parents, have *paid* for the fantasy. The parameters of the game are already in place, just as the trajectory of a girl's life is already announced. And a significant part of that trajectory is the idea that life requires accessories, that no act of fantasy is complete unless you buy the right pieces.

Parents receive, on the other hand, an illusion of control over the forces that shape their daughters' lives. It is comforting to feel that your daughter plays with history, and not the other way around. The glossy, gorgeous catalog, which comes four times a year, offers a good example of the "virtual gaze"—"a received *perception* mediated through representation." In this catalog history is miniaturized, made diminutive and unthreatening. If you have the money to buy it, it is yours, and you can give it to your daughter. Certainly this is a benevolent fantasy, and if it teaches your daughter that she matters, that she makes a difference in the scheme of things, it will probably do no harm.

But, finally, playing with Felicity or Molly or even Addy is really no different from playing with Barbie; Barbie—also accompanied by many accessories—has the equal potential to subvert oppressive notions of femininity.[23] Moreover, it is problematic to find ourselves living in a world where some girls play with $88 Addy dolls and some girls play with $8 Barbies. In our choice of toys, as in our choice of so many other consumer goods, we move increasingly toward a stratified society, in which competing notions of femininity are the source of division among different classes of women. Last, we need to be certain that we do not mistake buying a progressive doll for teaching our daughters—and sons—the real meaning of activism. While consumer practices can lead toward a sense of self-importance, toward the confidence to believe in one's self as an active participant in cultural process, that sense of empowerment must be directed outward, toward a commitment to righting social injustice. *All* little girls need to be taught that they have the power to make history and the responsibility to use that power to help others.

In the end there is no Western understanding of femininity that is not already embedded in the discourses of consumerism. This has been a book about the paradoxical construction of femininity in relation to those discourses. Disciplined or disruptive, controlled or unruly, the female consumer has resisted the cultural narrative that would contain her. She has thwarted the effort to suppress her speech and her desires. In her resistance we can locate a female-identified power that might disrupt the orderly conduct of business. Since we cannot deny or escape the fact that the female subject is constituted in relation to consumption, we might acknowledge it and make it the basis of our critique. Let us use what consumer culture gives us: if, for example, women consumers are targeted as "important," let us take the sense of our own importance and redirect it toward an active engagement with social and political processes. If consumer culture urges us to make "significant" choices, let us take the illusion of choice and think about real choices, real decisions we might make that would alter the course of events. If consumer culture tells us that we are powerful agents, let us take that sense of agency and turn it into practice. Venus Xtravaganza teaches us an important lesson: even the most radical assertion of womanhood depends upon a prior definition of femininity that is always already rooted in a commodified understanding of gender. In response to Venus's tragic lesson, let us make our own commodity a force with which to reckon.

Notes

Introduction

1. Tobias Smollett, *The Expedition of Humphry Clinker* (Oxford: Oxford University Press, 1991 [1771]). Further references are cited parenthetically.

2. Indeed, it is worth remembering that Smollett has long been assumed to be one of the great "comic" novelists.

3. Two recent analyses touching upon the theme of female consumption in this novel are James P. Carson, "Commodification and the Figure of the Castrato in Smollett's *Humphry Clinker*," *The Eighteenth Century: Theory and Interpretation* (1992), 33:24–46; and Charlotte Sussman, "Lismahago's Captivity": Transculturation in *Humphry Clinker*, ELH (1994), 61:597–618.

4. C. Willett and Phillis Cunnington, *Handbook of English Costume in the Eighteenth Century* (London: Faber and Faber, 1957), p. 383.

5. As Carson points out, in the novel the "figure of the castrato can serve as a valuable index of the gynophobic nature of Smollett's critique of the social and economic changes he perceives." Carson, "Commodification," p. 25.

6. See Sussman, "Lismahago's Captivity," pp. 613–14, for a reading of Tabitha's role in a process of "intercultural contact."

7. One could explain this connection any number of ways. The anthropologist Sherry Ortner, for example, hypothesizes that the origin of the almost universal association between women and bodily process lies in woman's " 'natural' association with the domestic context." In addition, "because of the animal-like nature of children, and because of the infrasocial connotation of the domestic group as against the rest of society," women have become aligned with the natural and with the body: "Is Female to Male as Nature Is to Culture?" in Michelle Zimbalist Rosaldo and Louise Lamphere, eds., *Women, Culture, and Society* (Stanford: Stanford University Press, 1974), p. 80. For a psychoanalytic account of the cultural linkage between women and the body, one could

also see Dorothy Dinnerstein, *The Mermaid and the Minotaur: Sexual Arrangement and the Human Malaise* (New York: Harper and Row, 1976). For a discussion of how, under the rubric of Western medical science—and under a humoral science in particular—women have been troped by their body parts, see Gail Kern Paster, *The Body Embarrassed: Drama and the Disciplines of Shame in Early Modern England* (Ithaca: Cornell University Press, 1993). Where issues of boundary and bodily integrity were crucial, argues Paster, the female body has been thought to "leak," to threaten and challenge containment.

8. Plato, *Timeus*, trans. Francis M. Cornford (Indianapolis: Bobbs-Merrill, 1959), p. 115.

9. Patricia Parker, *Literary Fat Ladies: Rhetoric, Gender, Property* (New York: Methuen, 1987), p. 26. See the picture of a scold's bridle, as Parker describes it, "a kind of chastity belt for the tongue," on p. 27.

10. See Susan Bordo, *Unbearable Weight: Feminism, Western Culture, and the Body* (Berkeley: University of California Press, 1993), especially "Hunger as Ideology."

11. See Mary Douglas and Baron Isherwood, *The World of Goods* (New York: Basic, 1979); and Grant McCracken, *Culture and Consumption: New Approaches to the Symbolic Character of Consumer Goods and Activities* (Bloomington: Indiana University Press, 1988). For review essays discussing the range of possible responses to consumer culture, see Mica Nava, "Consumerism and Its Contradictions," *Cultural Studies* (1987), 1:204–10; and Christopher Lasch, "The Culture of Consumption," in Mary Kupiec Cayton, Elliot J. Korn, and Peter Williams, eds., *Encyclopedia of American Social History*, 3 vols. (New York: Scribners, 1993), 2:1381–1390. The term *consumer culture* signals that the interpreter is receptive to the many creative uses that consumers make of their goods. Among the leftists who concede that consumerism may be multidimensional in its meaning is Judith Williamson, who concedes, "Consuming products does give a thrill, a sense of both belonging and being different, charging normality with the thrill of excitement of the unusual," in *Consuming Passions: The Dynamics of Popular Culture* (London: Boyars, 1985), p. 13.

12. McCracken, *Culture and Consumption*, p. 19, paraphrasing the work of Russell Belk.

13. I summarize briefly the well-known argument of the first chapter of Neil McKendrick, John Brewer, and J. H. Plumb, eds., *The Birth of a Consumer Society: The Commercialization of Eighteenth-Century England* (Bloomington: Indiana University Press, 1982), pp. 10, 11, 14.

14. McCracken, *Culture and Consumption*, p. 22. For a related argument about how "romantic teachings" provided a necessary motivation for consumer society to take hold, see Colin Campbell, *The Romantic Ethic and the Spirit of Modern Consumerism* (London: Blackwell, 1987).

15. Carole Shammas, *The Pre-industrial Consumer in England and America* (Oxford: Clarendon, 1990); Lorna Weatherill, *Consumer Behavior and Material Culture in Britain, 1660–1770* (Cambridge: Cambridge University Press, 1988); Beverly Lemire, *Fashion's Favourite: The Cotton Trade and the Consumer in Britain* (Oxford: Oxford University Press, 1991).

16. See, for example, Jean Christophe Agnew, "Coming Up for Air: Consumer Culture in Historical Perspective," *Intellectual History Newsletter* (1990), 12:3–21. Reprinted in John Brewer and Roy Porter, eds., *Consumption and the World of Goods* (New York: Routledge, 1993), pp. 19–39.

17. See Brewer and Porter, *Consumption and the World of Goods*.

18. Brewer and Porter, "Introduction," *Consumption and the World of Goods*. See also Roy Porter's essay in the collection, entitled, "Consumption: Disease of the Consumer Society?" pp. 58–81.

19. Fanny Burney, *Cecilia*, ed. Margaret Anne Doody and Peter Sabor (New York: Oxford University Press, 1990 [1782]), p. 193.

20. Louis Landa, "Of Silkworms and Farthingales and the Will of God," in R. F. Brissenden, ed., *Studies in the Eighteenth Century*, 2 vols. (Toronto: the University of Toronto, 1973), p. 277. See also his essay "Pope's Belinda, The General Emporie of the World, and the Wondrous Worm," *South Atlantic Quarterly* (1971), 70:215–35.

21. On the contradictions inherent in "economic theodicy," see John Barrell and Harriet Guest, "On the Use of Contradiction: Economics and Contradiction in the Eighteenth-Century Long Poem," in Felicity Nussbaum and Laura Brown, eds., *The New Eighteenth Century* (New York: Methuen 1987), pp. 121–43.

22. T. E. Jessop, *The Works of George Berkeley, Bishop of Cloyne*, 8 vols. (London: Thomas Nelson, 1953), 6:117.

23. Bernard Mandeville, remark T, *Fable of the Bees*, ed. Phillip Harth (New York: Penguin, 1970 [1714]), p. 237.

24. Ibid., pp. 237–38.

25. Ibid., p. 238.

26. On this subject, see also Laura Brown's analysis in chapter 6 of *Ends of Empire: Women and Ideology in Early Eighteenth-Century Literature* (Ithaca: Cornell University Press, 1993), pp. 170–200.

27. Jonathan Swift, "A Letter to the Archbishop of Dublin, Concerning the Weavers," in Herbert Davis, ed., *Irish Tracts, 1728–1733* (Oxford: Basil Blackwell, 1971), p. 67.

28. Swift, "A Letter to the Archbishop," p. 68.

29. Jonathan Swift, "A Proposal That All the Ladies and Women of Ireland Should Appear Constantly in Irish Manufacturers," in Herbert Davis, ed., *Irish Tracts, 1728–1733* (Oxford: Basil Blackwell, 1971), p. 126.

30. And elsewhere Swift does elaborate on how English economic policy results in the depletion of Irish resources. See "A Short View of the State of Ireland," reprinted in Davis, *Irish Tracts*. It is interesting to note that when Swift discusses the possibility of raising taxes on imported wine, a product consumed more frequently by men, he provides reasons why this should not occur, among them that Ireland would lose "gentlemen of tolerable estates" and Irish "are in more want of some cordial, to keep up their spirits. . . . I am not in jest." "A Proposal," p. 125. So the importing of commodities used by men does not seem to have bothered Swift as much as the importing of commodities appreciated by women.

31. For a discussion of shopping in *Marriage* and *Camilla*, see "Shopping" in this volume. The citation from *Sanditon* appears in Margaret Drabble, ed., *Lady Susan, The Watsons, Sanditon* (New York: Penguin, 1974), p. 178.

32. Nancy Armstrong, "Occidental Alice," *differences: A Journal of Feminist Cultural Studies* (1990), 2(2):17.

33. I disagree with Armstrong's contention that Lewis Carroll's Alice "feels anxious about a desire that earlier generations simply could not have felt" ("Occidental Alice," p. 17). To the contrary, I argue that women were well acquainted with the dangers of their own "desires" long before the appearance of the department store, as Armstrong maintains. See the work of Rachel

Bowlby for another discussion of the role of the department store in the cultural construction of female desire in *Just Looking: Consumer Culture in Dreiser, Gissing, and Zola* (New York: Methuen, 1985).

34. See Catherine Belsey, "Constructing the Subject, Deconstructing the Text," in Robyn Warhol and Diane Price Herndl, ed., *Feminisms* (New Brunswick: Rutgers University Press, 1991), pp. 593–609.

35. Mary Poovey, *The Proper Lady and the Woman Writer: Ideology as Style in the Works of Mary Woll-stonecraft, Mary Shelley, and Jane Austen* (Chicago: University of Chicago Press, 1984); Nancy Armstrong, *Desire and Domestic Fiction: A Political History of the Novel* (New York: Oxford University Press, 1987); Kathryn Shevelow, *Women and Print Culture: The Construction of Femininity in the Early Periodical* (New York: Routledge, 1989); Felicity Nussbaum, *The Autobiographical Subject: Gender and Ideology in Eighteenth-Century England* (Baltimore: Johns Hopkins University Press, 1989); and Laura Brown, *Ends of Empire: Women and Ideology in Early Eighteenth-Century English Literature* (Ithaca: Cornell University Press, 1993).

36. One especially helpful exploration of the usefulness of Foucault for feminism is Jana Sawicki, *Disciplining Foucault: Feminism, Power, and the Body* (New York: Routledge, 1991). But also see Bordo, who argues that feminists recognized the "docile" body long before Foucault (*Unbearable Weight*, p. 17).

37. See Thomas Laqueur, *Making Sex: Body and Gender from the Greeks to Freud* (Cambridge: Harvard University Press, 1990).

38. Michel Foucault, *Discipline and Punish: The Birth of the Prison*, trans. Alan Sheridan (New York: Random House, 1979), p. 26.

39. Mica Nava, "Consumerism and Its Contradictions," *Cultural Studies* (1987), 1:209.

40. Susan Douglas, *Where the Girls Are: Growing Up Female with the Mass Media* (New York: Times, 1994), p. 9.

Tea

1. Mary Elizabeth Braddon, *Lady Audley's Secret* (New York: Oxford University Press, 1987 [1862]), p. 222.

2. Elizabeth Cleghorn Gaskell, *North and South* (London: J. M. Dent, 1968 [1855]), p. 74.

3. See Michel Foucault, *Discipline and Punish: The Birth of the Prison*, trans. Alan Sheridan (New York: Random House, 1979).

4. *Encyclopedia Americana*, 30 vols. (Danbury, Ct. Grolier, 1991), 26:342. For a complete etymological history of the word *tea,* see William H. Ukers, *All About Tea*, 2 vols. (New York: Tea and Coffee Trade Journal, 1935), 1:492–95.

5. Agnes Repellier, *To Think of Tea!* (Boston: Houghton Mifflin, 1932), pp. 4 and 8. Also useful for a history of tea in English culture is Jason Godwin's *A Time for Tea: Travels Through China and India in Search of Tea* (New York: Knopf, 1991). Compare also Fernand Braudel, *The Structures of Everyday Life: The Limits of the Possible* (Harper and Row: 1979), pp. 249–60 (vol. 1 of *Civilization and Capitalism*).

6. Bruce Lenman, "The English and Dutch East India Companies and the Birth of Consumerism in the Augustan World," *Eighteenth-Century Life* (1990), 14:57.

7. K. N. Chaudhuri, *The Trading World of Asia and the East India Company* (Cambridge: Cambridge University Press, 1978), p. 388.

8. Agnes Strickland, *Lives of the Queens of England*, 8 vols. (London: Longmans, Green, Reader, and Dyer, 1871), 5:485.

9. Edmund Waller, *Works in Verse and Prose* (London: J. Tonson, 1729), p. 221.

10. At one point Catherine must have been surprised to hear that her husband considered a son born to him by Lady Castlemaine to be his heir. See Strickland, *Lives of the Queens*, p. 526.

11. For a full discussion of how women lost out on opportunities for work in the eighteenth century, see Bridget Hill, *Women, Work, and Sexual Politics in Eighteenth-Century England* (London: Basil Blackwell, 1989), as well as the discussion in the section of this volume entitled "Business."

12. William Congreve, *The Double Dealer*, in Alexander Charles Ewald, ed., *Complete Plays* (New York: Hill and Wang, 1956), act 1, scene i, p. 121.

13. See Jürgen Habermas, *The Structural Transformation of the Public Sphere*, trans. Thomas Berger (Cambridge: MIT Press, 1989). See also Lawrence Klein, "Gender, Conversation, and the Public Sphere in Early Eighteenth-Century England," in Michael Worten and Judith Still, ed., *Textuality and Sexuality* (Manchester: Manchester University Press, 1993), pp. 100–15.

14. Wolfang Schivelbusch, *Tastes of Paradise: A Social History of Spices, Stimulants, and Intoxicants*, trans. David Jacobson (New York: Pantheon, 1992), p. 19.

15. Ibid., pp. 37–38.

16. Peter Stallybrass and Allon White, *The Politics and Poetics of Transgression* (Ithaca: Cornell University Press, 1986), pp. 95, 96.

17. Ibid., p. 97.

18. According to Anne C. Wilson, Thomas Whiting opened the first tea shop for ladies in Devereux Court, London 1717. Still, for the most part, tea—unlike coffee—was the drink associated with home, the private and the domestic. See *Food and Drink in Britain from the Stone Age to Recent Times* (New York: Barnes and Noble, 1974), p. 413.

19. Peter Motteux, *A Poem in Praise of Tea* (London: J. Tonson, 1712).

20. Rodris Roth, "Tea-Drinking in Eighteenth-Century America: Its Etiquette and Equipage," in Robert Blair St. George, ed., *Material Life in America, 1600–1860* (Boston: Northeastern University Press, 1988), p. 444. The gendering of tea as "feminine" appears to have been particularly Western, since in Asian cultures such as that of Japan, the Cha No Yu (tea ceremony) allows for tea masters of either gender.

21. Margaret Visser, *The Rituals of Dinner: The Origins, Evolution, Eccentricities, and Meaning of Table Manners* (New York: Grove Weidenfeld, 1991), p. 19. Though Visser writes little about the eighteenth-century British tea table, her insights about the importance and significance of food rituals provide a helpful overview for the subject.

22. Roth, "Tea-Drinking," p. 446, tells the story of one foreign visitor's bafflement over the correct placement of the spoon. Also, on the placement of the spoon, see Nancy Woodward, *Teas of the World* (New York: Collier, 1980), p. 115. Anne Wilson, *Food and Drink in Britain*, p. 413, also refers to the ceremonial aspects of tea drinking.

23. Sherry B. Ortner, "Is Female to Male as Nature Is to Culture?" in Michelle Zimbalist Ros-

aldo and Louise Lamphere, eds., *Woman, Culture, and Society* (Stanford: Stanford University Press, 1974), p. 80.

24. I paraphrase here from Foucault, *Discipline and Punish*, p. 138.

25. For the response of one servant to upper-class snobbery about working-class pretensions, see Elizabeth Hands, "A Poem, On the Supposition of an Advertisement Appearing in a Morning Paper, of the Publication of a Volume of Poems, by a Servant-Maid," in Roger Lonsdale, ed., *Eighteenth-Century Women Poets: An Oxford Anthology* (New York: Oxford University Press, 1989), p. 4. This poem provides an immediate sense of what the tea table might have looked like from the servant's perspective.

26. [Richard Steele], *Spectator*, no. 552, ed. Donald Bond, 5 vols. (Oxford: Clarendon Press, 1965), 4:479.

27. William Cowper, "The Task," book 4, "The Winter Evening," in H. S. Milford, ed., *The Poetical Works of William Cowper* (London: Oxford University Press, 1950), p. 182.

28. Neil McKendrick, "Josiah Wedgwood and the Commercialization of the Potteries," in Neil McKendrick, John Brewer, and J.H. Plumb, eds., *The Birth of a Consumer Society: The Commercialization of Eighteenth-Century England* (Bloomington: Indiana University Press, 1982), p. 76.

29. Eliza Haywood, *The Tea Table, or A Conversation Between Some Polite Persons of Both Sexes at a Lady's Visiting Day* (London: J. Roberts, 1725), p. 1.

30. Edward Young, "Love of Fame, the Universal Passion," 6th satire, in *The Poetical Works of Edward Young,* 2 vols. (Boston: Little, Brown, 1854), 2:134.

31. For more on Jonas Hanway and the construction of maternity, see Ruth Perry, "Colonizing the Breast: Sexuality and Maternity in Eighteenth-Century England," *Journal of the History of Sexuality* (1991), 2:207–10.

32. Jonas Hanway, "An Essay on Tea," *A Journal of Eight Days Journey*, 2 vols. (London: Woodfell and Hendersen, 1757), vol. 2. Further references are cited parenthetically.

33. His argument is in fact similar to that of Duncan Forbes, who makes many of the same points regarding the effect of importing tea on the Scottish economy, in *Some Considerations on the Present State of Scotland*, 3d ed. (Edinburgh: Sands, Murray, Cochran, 1764).

34. See Louis Landa, "Of Silkworms and Farthingales and the Will of God," in R. F. Brissenden, ed., *Studies in the Eighteenth Century*, 2 vols. (Toronto: University of Toronto, 1973), 2:259–77.

35. Hanway's obsession with the "emasculating" effects of tea might be read against John Sekora's discussion of the effects of luxury in the works of Tobias Smollett. See *Luxury: The Concept in Western Thought, Eden to Smollett* (Baltimore: Johns Hopkins University Press, 1977).

36. See Kathleen Wilson, *The Sense of the People: Politics, Culture, and Imperialism in England, 1715–1785* (New York: Cambridge University Press, 1995).

37. Simon Pauli, *A Treatise on Tobacco, Tea, Coffee, and Chocolate*, trans. D. Jones (London: T. Osborne, 1746), p. 142.

38. [Samuel Johnson], "Review of *Eight Days Journey*," in *The Literary Magazine or Universal Review*, 2 vols. (London: J. Wilkie, 1757), 2(xiii):163.

39. For another polemic against the dangers of wet-nursing, see the *Spectator*, 2(246):454–56.

40. John Coakley Lettsom, *The Natural History of the Tea Table* (London: Charles Dilly, 1799), p. 89.

41. [Eliza Haywood], *The Female Spectator*, 4 vols. (London: T. Gardner, 1745), 2:96. For a precise calculation of the cost of tea relative to the income of a working family later in the century, see Lettsom, *The Natural History*, p. 100.

42. See Perry, "Colonizing the Breast."

43. Simon Mason, *The Good and Bad Effects of Tea Considered* (London: M. Cooper, 1745). Cf. Dr. Johnson: "Tea is not a liquor proper for the lower classes of the people, as it supplies no strength to labour, or relief to disease, but gratifies the taste without nourishing the body." "Review of *Eight Day's Journey*," p. 166.

Sugar

1. Aileen Dawson, *Masterpieces of Wedgwood in the British Museum* Bloomington: Indiana University Press, 1984), pp. 45, 63.

2. Louise Fagan Yellin, *Women and Sister: The Antislavery Feminists in American Culture* (New Haven: Yale University Press, 1989), p. 8. Yellin is paraphrasing the words of Thomas Clarkson, an abolitionist leader and historian.

3. Hélène Cixous, "Sorties," *The Newly Born Woman*, trans. Betsy Wing (Minneapolis: University of Minnesota Press, 1986), p. 90.

4. Ruth Salvaggio, *Enlightened Absences: Neoclassical Configurations of the Feminine* (Urbana: University of Illinois Press, 1988), pp. 14, 26.

5. For a fascinating discussion of women as leaky vessels in seventeenth-century drama, see Gail Kern Paster, *The Body Embarrassed: Drama and the Disciplines of Shame in Early Modern England* (Ithaca: Cornell University Press, 1993), chapter 2.

6. Cited by Sidney W. Mintz in *Sweetness and Power: The Place of Sugar in Modern History* (New York: Viking Penguin, 1985), p. 106.

7. See Sidney W. Mintz, "Sweet, Salt, and the Language of Love," *Modern Language Notes* (1991), 106:859.

8. Moira Ferguson, *Subject to Others: British Women Writers and Colonial Slavery, 1670–1834* (New York: Routledge, 1992), p. 182–83.

9. Clare Midgley, *Women Against Slavery: The British Campaigns, 1780–1870* (London: Routledge, 1992), pp. 35, 40.

10. Deirdre Coleman, "Conspicuous Consumption: White Abolitionism and English Women's Protest Writing in the 1790s" *ELH* (1994), 61:345.

11. Charlotte Sussman, "Women and the Politics of Sugar, 1792," *Representations* (1994), 48:65.

12. Mary Birkett, *A Poem on the African Slave Trade: Addressed to Her Own Sex* (Dublin: J. Jones, 1792).

13. Laura Brown, *Ends of Empire: Women and Ideology in Early Eighteenth-Century English Literature* (Ithaca: Cornell, 1993), pp. 116–17.

14. Coleman, "Conspicuous Consumption," p. 353.

15. Mary Wollstonecraft, *A Vindication of the Rights of Woman*, ed. Carol H. Poston (New York: Norton, 1975 [1792]), p. 145.

16. Adam Smith, *The Wealth of the Nations*, ed. Andrew Skinner, books 1–3 (New York: Penguin, 1986 [1776]), p. 182.

17. Jane Austen, *Mansfield Park* (New York: Penguin, 1966 [1814]), p. 55. As Maaja Stewart writes, "Lady Bertram bears an uncanny resemblance to planters' wives in the West Indies": *Domestic Realities and Imperial Fictions: Jane Austen's Novels in Eighteenth-Century Contexts* (Athens: University of Georgia Press, 1993), p. 129.

18. William Cowper, "The Negro's Complaint," *The Poetical Works of William Cowper*, ed. H. S. Milford (London: Oxford University Press, 1950), pp. 371–72.

19. William Fox, *An Address to the People of Great Britain on the Propriety of Abstaining from West Indian Sugar and Rum* (London: R. Gurney, 1791).

20. Benjamin Moseley, *A Treatise on Sugar with Miscellaneous Medical Observations*, 2d ed. (London: John Nichols, 1800).

21. Ibid., p. 144.

22. Going in another direction, one might also think about the Eucharistic symbolism of drinking the slave's blood. Coleman, "Conspicuous Consumption," p. 349, for example, describes an abolitionist cartoon by Gillray in which a black African becomes a type of crucified Christ. However, because of Birkett's Quaker roots, this connection seems more difficult to assert.

23. In Sterne's text the line reads, "Disguise thyself as thou wilt, still slavery! said I—still thou art a bitter draught": *A Sentimental Journey Through France and Italy*, ed. Graham Petrie (New York: Penguin, 1975 [1768]), p. 96. Birkett appears to have been keen to emphasize the word *cup*.

24. Julia Kristeva, *Powers of Horror: An Essay on Abjection*, trans. Leon S. Roudiez (New York: Columbia University Press, 1982), p. 71.

25. Danielle Jacquart and Claude Thomasset, *Sexuality and Medicine in the Middle Ages*, trans. Matthew Adamson (Princeton: Princeton University Press, 1985), p. 73.

26. Patricia Crawford, "Attitudes to Menstruation in Seventeenth-Century England, *Past and Present*, (1981), 91:59.

27. Ibid., p. 61.

28. Paster, *The Body Embarrassed*, p. 81.

29. Ibid., p. 83.

30. See Barbara Bush, *Slave Women in Caribbean Society, 1650—1838* (Bloomington: Indiana University Press, 1990).

China

1. Alexander Pope, *The Rape of the Lock*, in Geoffrey Tillotson, ed., *The Poems of Alexander Pope*, 11 volumes (New Haven: Yale University Press, 1961–1969), vol. 3, canto 2, lines 105–6, and canto 3, lines 157–60. My thinking about this topic is indebted to Aubrey Williams's essay, "The 'Fall' of China and *The Rape of the Lock*," *Philological Quarterly* (1962), 41:412–25. On Pope's treatment of Belinda as object of male desire and ownership, see Ellen Pollak, *The Poetics of Sexual Myth: Gender and Ideology in the Verse of Swift and Pope* (Chicago: University of Chicago Press, 1985), pp. 77–107. On the theme of "reification" in *The Rape of the Lock*, see C. E. Nicholson, "A World of Artefacts: *The Rape of the Lock* as Social History," *Literature and History* (1979), pp. 183–93.

2. Laura Brown, "Reading Race and Gender: Jonathan Swift," *Eighteenth-Century Studies* (1990): 424–443.

3. Cleanth Brooks: "Pope does not say, but he suggests, that chastity is, like the fine porcelain,

something brittle, precious, useless, and easily broken." See *The Well Wrought Urn* (New York: Harcourt Brace, 1947), p. 87.

4. Laura Brown, *Ends of Empire:Women and Ideology in Early Eighteenth-Century English Literature* (Ithaca: Cornell University Press, 1993), pp. 119 and 112.

5. Ibid., pp. 119 and 112.

6. Ibid., p. 112. The essentialism to which the phrase refers belongs to the period, not Brown.

7. See, for example, Samuel Johnson, "The Rambler," February 15, 1752, no. 200, in Walter Jackson Bate and Albrecht Strauss, eds., *The Works of Samuel Johnson,* 16 vols. (New Haven: Yale University Press, 1969–90), 3:277–281. Or, a little later, see Charles Lamb on his "feminine partiality" for "Old China," *Life, Letters,Writing of Charles Lamb*, ed. Percy Fitzgerald, 6 vols. (London: T. and A. Constable, 1892), vi:118–25.

8. Lorna Weatherill, *Consumer Behavior and Material Culture in Britain, 1660–1770* (Cambridge: Cambridge University Press, 1988), p. 31.

9. According to the *The Compact Edition of the Oxford English Dictionary*, one definition of *china* is "a species of earthenware of fine semi-transparent texture, originally manufactured in China and brought to Europe in the sixteenth century by the Portuguese, who named it porcelain." What specifically distinguishes porcelain from other types of china is a particular kind of clay called kaolin. See *The Compact Edition of the Oxford English Dictionary*, 2 vols. (New York: Oxford University Press, 1971), 1:351.

10. It is to be noted that chinoiserie encompasses a range of materials in addition to porcelain, including textiles and paintings. The *Oxford Companion to Art* defines *chinoiserie* as "properly a European style in the arts and crafts reflecting fanciful and poetic notions of China which from the time of Marco Polo have been conjured up from travelers' tales and from exports of ceramics, textiles, and *objets d'art*. See Harold Osborne, ed., *The Oxford Companion to Art* (Oxford: Oxford University Press, 1970), p. 236.

11. J. H. Plumb, "The Royal Porcelain Craze," *In the Light of History* (Boston: Houghton Mifflin, 1973), pp. 59 and 58.

12. See Ben Jonson, *Epicoene, or The Silent Woman*: "To watch when ladies are gone to the china-houses, or the Exchange, that he may meet them by chance" (act 1, scene i), in *The Complete Plays of Ben Jonson*, 2 vols. (New York: Dutton, 1919), 1:497.

13. Eric Jones, "The Fashion Manipulators: Consumer Tastes and British Industries, 1660–1800" in Louis Cain and Paul Uselding, eds., *Business Enterprise and Economic Change* (Kent State: Kent State University Press, 1973), p. 205.

14. William Wycherley, *The Country Wife,* act 4, scene iii, in John Harold Wilson, ed., *Six Restoration Plays* (Boston: Houghton Mifflin, 1959), p. 60.

15. Joseph Addison, "The Lover," Thursday, March 18, 1714, no. 10, in George Washington Greene, ed., *The Works of Joseph Addison*, 5 vols. (New York: Putnam, 1853), 3:866.

16. Carole Shammas, *The Pre-Industrial Consumer in England and America* (Oxford: Clarendon Press, 1990), pp. 187 and 192n.

17. Lorna Weatherill, "A Possession of One's Own: Women and Consumer Behavior in England, 1660–1740," *Journal of British Studies* (1986), 25:140.

18. Louis Landa, "Of Silkworms and Farthingales and the Will of God," in R. F. Brissenden,

ed., *Studies in the Eighteenth Century*, 2 vols. (Toronto: University of Toronto Press, 1973), p. 262.

19. *The Compact Edition of the OED*, 1:351.

20. On the British acquisition of the Indian trading routes as part of Catherine's dowry, see Gertrude Z. Thomas, *Richer Than Spices* (New York: Knopf, 1965), especially chapters 1–3.

21. Ibid., chapter 8, "The Porcelain Mystery."

22. Neil McKendrick, "Josiah Wedgwood and the Commercialization of the Potteries," in Neil McKendrick, John Brewer, and J. H. Plumb, eds., *The Birth of a Consumer Society: The Commercialization of Eighteenth-Century England* (Bloomington: University of Indiana Press, 1982), pp. 100–45; Thomas, *Richer Than Spices*, pp. 133–34.

23. See Edward Said, *Orientalism* (New York: Random House, 1979).

24. Lamb, *Life, Letters, Writing*, p. 118.

25. Geoffrey Godden, *British Pottery: An Illustrated Guide* (London: Barrie and Jenkins, 1974), p. 229. Godden explains the elements that are ubiquitously present in nineteenth-century blue willow ware and are present only irregularly in earlier eighteenth-century versions: "The salient features of the traditional English 'Willow pattern' design are buildings in the centre or to the right of centre, a prominent Willow tree and two or three figures crossing a bridge to the left, away from the building, two doves being normally placed in the sky above the fleeing lovers! A fence runs across the foreground, and a wide, ornate Chinese-styled border design encloses the whole." *Caughley and Worcester Porcelains, 1775–1800* (New York: Praeger, 1969), p. 15.

26. Godden, *Caughley and Worcester Porcelains*, p. 16.

27. Harriet Wynter, *An Introduction to European Porcelain* (London: Arlington, 1971), p. 191.

28. George Savage, *Porcelain Through the Ages* (Baltimore: Penguin, 1963), p. 261.

29. See Godden: "While the English manufacturers could not compete with the Chinese dinner services with their large dishes, heavy tureens and numerous plates, they could apparently compete with dessert and tea services, so that, while English blue and white dinner services are extremely rare, teawares comprise well over half the whole output of the Caughley factory." *Caughley and Worcester Porcelains*, p. 14.

30. Williams, "The 'Fall' of China," p. 418.

31. See Barbara McGovern, *Anne Finch and Her Poetry: A Critical Biography* (Athens: University of Georgia Press, 1992), pp. 136–43; and Charles H. Hinnant, "Feminism and Femininity: A Reconsideration of Anne Finch's 'Ardelia's Answer to Ephelia,' " *The Eighteenth Century: Theory and Interpretation* (1992), 33:119–32.

32. Anne Finch, Countess of Winchilsea, "Ardelia's Answer to Ephelia," in Katherine M. Rogers and William McCarthy, eds., *The Meridien Anthology of Early Women Writers: British Literary Women from Aphra Behn to Maria Edgeworth* (New York: Penguin, 1987), pp. 85–92.

33. McGovern, *Anne Finch and Her Poetry*, p. 140.

34. Ann Messenger, in an essay entitled "Publishing Without Perishing: Lady Winchelsea's *Miscellany Poems of 1713*," finds most of Winchelsea's poems written before 1703 and 1709 "critical of women." *Restoration* (1981), 5:30.

35. Hinnant argues that the poem resists the kind of essentialism that pervades Rochester's misogyny, targeting instead a particular "construction" of femininity: "Almeria's attributes are not

seen as 'natural,' but are shown rather as the result of a highly particularized cultural transformation of sexuality into gender." In addition, he points out that neither is Ardelia the more "natural" (or essential) representation, despite her alignment with the "natural" virtues of the country: "Ardelia's 'rustick cloaths and meen' are meant to be understood not as a more 'natural' representation of femininity but rather as a studied and more self-conscious alternative to [the misogynist ideology implicit in Rochester's poem]. They are the means by which Finch constructs herself, under the coterie name of Ardelia, as Almeria's opposite." "Feminism and Femininity," pp. 127 and 130.

36. Fanny Burney, *Camilla, Or a Picture of Youth* (New York: Oxford University Press, 1983 [1796]), p. 151.

37. What Armstrong has to say about the invention of "depth" in the female subject during the latter decades of the eighteenth century seems highly relevant to this novel. See Nancy Armstrong, *Desire and Domestic Fiction: A Political History of the Novel* (New York: Oxford University Press, 1987), pp. 75–76. However, as I have been suggesting all along, the criterion of depth is present much earlier in the century as well. See Margaret Doody for a reading of the role of the male viewer in the novel: *Frances Burney: The Life in the Works* (New Brunswick: Rutgers University Press, 1988), chapter 6.

38. Feminist critics remain at odds on the question of how to read the spectacular ending of this novel. In addition to Doody, see Kristina Straub, *Divided Fictions: Fanny Burney and Feminine Strategy* (Lexington: University of Kentucky Press, 1987), chapter 7; or Julia Epstein, *The Iron Pen: Frances Burney and the Politics of Women's Writing* (Madison: University of Wisconsin Press, 1989), chapter 4.

39. Susan Ferrier, *Marriage* (New York: Penguin, 1986 [1818]), pp. 138–39.

40. On the particular dynamics of scapegoating the female, see Laura Mandell, "Bawds and Merchants: Engendering Capitalist Desires" *ELH* (1992), 59:109–11.

41. Mary Douglas and Baron Isherwood, *The World of Goods* (New York: Basic, 1979), p. 66.

42. Luce Irigaray, "The 'Mechanics' of Fluids," in *This Sex Which Is Not One*, trans. Catherine Porter (Ithaca: Cornell University Press, 1985), p. 112.

Introduction: Commodities

1. George Birkbeck Hill, ed., *Boswell's Life of Johnson*, 6 vols. 2d ed., revised by I. F. Powell (Oxford: Clarendon Press, 1964), 5:442. The editor supplies the missing "no."

2. *The Compact Edition of the Oxford English Dictionary*, 2 vols. (Oxford: Oxford University Press, 1971), 1:482.

3. Any work on women as commodities would begin with Gayle Rubin's seminal essay, which responds to the work of Levi-Strauss, "The Traffic in Women: Notes on the 'Political Economy' of Sex," in Rayna Reiter, ed., *Toward an Anthropology of Women* (New York: Monthly Review, 1975), pp. 157–210. Also crucial is the work of Luce Irigaray, *The Sex Which Is Not One*, trans. Catherine Porter (Ithaca: Cornell University Press, 1985). For a critique of how such theoretical approaches assume "untroubled unified subjects exchanging women/objects" see Karen Newman, "Directing Traffic: Subjects, Objects, and the Politics of Exchange," *Differences* (1990), 2:41–54.

4. John Brewer, Neil McKendrick, and J. H. Plumb are, of course, to be credited with bring-

ing to our attention the importance of consumerism to the eighteenth century. See *The Birth of a Consumer Society: The Commercialization of Eighteenth-Century England* (Bloomington: Indiana University Press, 1982); and, more recently, John Brewer and Roy Porter, ed., *Consumption and the World of Goods* (New York: Routledge, 1993), which is the first of a projected three volumes.

5. Rachel Bowlby, *Just Looking: Consumer Culture in Dreiser, Gissing, and Zola* (New York: Methuen, 1985), p. 1.

6. John Stow, *A Survey of the Cities of London and Westminster*, cited by Karen Newman in "City Talk: Woman and Communication in Jonson's *Epicoene*," *ELH* (1989), 56:503–4.

7. Other historians similarly trace the origins of modern retail practice to the eighteenth, not the nineteenth, century. See Beverly Lemire: "One cannot look to the eighteenth century and expect to find the cumulative effects of an industrialization and mechanization characteristic of the next hundred years. Nevertheless, the eighteenth century witnessed the birth of entirely new elements in production and marketing: an unprecedented popular demand was founded on a popular appetite for new sorts of consumer goods apparent first in the late sixteenth and seventeenth centuries. The accomplishments of the eighteenth-century entrepreneurs in serving this first mass market cannot be discounted. The qualitative structure of the mass market was established prior to the Industrial Revolution. To claim the second half of the nineteenth century as the period of the mass market is short-sighted; observing the heavy flowering of that era, it ignores the roots and branches from which that prosperity sprung." *Fashion's Favorite: The Cotton Trade and Consumer in Britain, 1660–1800* (Oxford: Oxford University Press, 1991), pp. 198–99.

8. The phrase belongs to Greimas, as cited by Ronald Schleifer, "Introduction," *Structural Semiotics*, trans. Danielle McDowell, Ronald Schleifer, and Alan Velie (Lincoln: University of Nebraska Press, 1966), p. xv. Though redeemed by Jameson in *The Political Unconscious*, Greimas's semiotic square continues to suffer from Jonathan Culler's critique in *Structuralist Poetics* (Ithaca: Cornell University Press, 1975); see esp. p. 85. Still, I would argue that the value of this tool lies in its descriptive powers. Here I offer not the "meaning" of a cultural shift but one possible understanding of that shift. For a discussion of the usefulness of the semiotic square in the analysis of character, see Nancy Armstrong, "Inside Greimas's Square: Literary Characters and Cultural Constraints," in Wendy Steiner, ed., *The Sign in Music and Literature* (Austin: University of Texas Press, 1981), pp. 52–66.

9. Schleifer, "Introduction," p. xxxi, explains the significance of this sequential dimension of Greimas's square: "It situates semantics in time as a function of discourse in ways that phonology is not so situated."

10. As before, I take my definition from the *OED*, though John Sekora's work continues to be the definitive source on attitudes toward luxury in the eighteenth century. See *Luxury: The Concept in Western Thought from Eden to Smollett* (Baltimore: Johns Hopkins University Press, 1974), especially chapters 3 and 4.

11. Cf. Anne Friedberg, who argues, " "To shop: as a verb, it implies choice, empowerment in the relation between looking and having, the act of buying as willful choice." See *Window Shopping: Cinema and the Postmodern* (Berkeley: University of California Press, 1993), p. 57.

12. Carole Shammas, *The Pre-Industrial Consumer in England and America* (New York: Oxford University Press, 1990), p. 259.

13. Cf. Sidney W. Mintz: "The growth in the consumption of sucrose and the stimulant beverages among the English people probably marks the first time in history that marketed edible luxuries were turned into everyday necessities." See "The Changing Roles of Food in the Study of Consumption," in Brewer and Porter, *Consumption and the World of Goods*, p. 261.

Shops and Shoppers

1. Hoh-Cheung Mui and Lorna H. Mui, *Shops and Shopkeeping in Eighteenth-Century England* (Montreal: McGill University Press, 1989), p. 27.

2. Jean-Christophe Agnew, *Worlds Apart: The Market and the Theatre in Anglo-American Thought, 1550–1750* (Cambridge: Cambridge University Press, 1986), p. 25.

3. Ibid., p. 41.

4. Dorothy Davis, *Fairs, Shops, and Supermarkets* (Toronto: University of Toronto Press, 1966), p. 20.

5. Cited by Davis, ibid., p. 102. Davis does not locate the exact moment when shopping became an "indoor" activity. She also cites the Quaker shopkeeper William Stout, as recorded in Pepys's diary, who remembers as a young man of seventeen dealing over the counter in the freezing cold of winter (p. 152). As late as the time of Defoe, "sales across open windows were still very common" (p. 191), though it would appear that sales increasingly took place indoors over the course of the century.

6. Ibid., p. 196.

7. Ibid., p. 192.

8. On the place of haggling for prices in England, as opposed to France, see Alison Adburgham, *Shops and Shopping, 1800–1914* (London: Allen and Unwin, 1964), p. 141. Adburgham argues that it became necessary to affix prices once the shopkeeper employed several assistants and could no longer rely on their bargaining skill as well as his own.

9. Davis, *Fairs, Shops, and Supermarkets*, p. 182.

10. Davis, ibid., p. 102. See also the *Spectator*, February 18, 1712, no. 304, for a satiric description of two different ways of attracting customers in the early eighteenth century. While the "Fawners . . . receive Passengers with a submissive Bow, and repeat with a gentle Voice, *Ladies what do you want? pray look in here*, the Worriers reach out their Hands at Pistol-Shot, and seize the Customers at Arm's length." Donald Bond, ed., *Spectator*, 5 vols. (Oxford: Oxford University Press, 1965), 3:95. Note that in both situations the seller leans out into the street.

11. In thinking about this issue I have found Beth Fowkes Tobin's discussion of the professionalism of the middle-class agent useful. See her book, *Superintending the Poor: Charitable Ladies and Paternal Lordlords in British Fiction, 1970–1860* (New Haven: Yale University Press, 1993). The Kress Collection of the Baker Library at the Harvard Business School contains a wide sample of this literature. Especially notable are the following: *The General Shop Book or the Tradesman's Universal Director* (London, 1753); William Markham, *A General Introduction to Trade and Business or The Young Merchant's and Tradesman's Magazine* (London: Bettesworth and Hitch, 1739); Malachy Postlethwayt and James Royson, *The British Mercantile Academy or The Accomplishing Merchant* (London: John and Paul Knapton, 1750); Peter Hudson, *A New Introduction to Trade and Business* (London, 1758); and R. Campbell, *The London Tradesman* (London: T. Gardner, 1747). Also instructive

is *A Letter from a Hawker and Peddler to a Member of Parliament*, a polemic that Charts the rise and fall of a young tradesman who is ruined through contact with unscrupulous peers.

12. Daniel Defoe, *The Complete English Tradesman in Familiar Letters*, 2 vols. (London: Charles Rivington, 1726–1727). Further references are cited parenthetically.

13. Bond, *Spectator*, 3:245.

14. Ibid.

15. R. Campbell, *The London Tradesman* (London: T. Gardner, 1747), p. 197.

16. See also Erin Mackie's work on the gendering of retail space, especially chapter 2 of her book *Fashion as Cultural Discourse: Commodity, Style, and Gender in the Tatler and Spectator Papers* (Baltimore: Johns Hopkins University Press, forthcoming).

17. See section 3, "Pornography."

18. Rachel Bowlby, *Just Looking: Consumer Culture in Dresier, Gissing, and Zola* (New York: Methuen, 1985), p. 32.

19. Bernard Mandeville, "A Search Into the Nature of Society" in Phillip Harth, ed., *The Fable of the Bees* (New York: Penguin, 1970), p. 353. Further references are cited parenthetically.

20. Bowlby, *Just Looking*, p. 20.

21. Samuel Richardson, *Clarissa, Or the History of a Young Lady*, ed. Angus Ross (New York: Penguin, 1988 [1747–1748]), p. 970. Further references are cited parenthetically.

22. John Richetti, "Lovelace Goes Shopping at Smith's: Power, Pay, and Class Privilege in *Clarissa*," *Studies in the Literary Imagination* (1995), 28:30.

23. Frances Burney, *Evelina* (New York: Oxford University Press, 1982 [1778]), p. 27.

24. *The Compact Edition of the Oxford English Dictionary*, 2 vols. (Oxford: Oxford University Press, 1971), 2:738.

25. Fanny Burney, *Camilla, Or a Picture of Youth* (New York: Oxford University Press, 1983 [1796]), p. 607. Further references are cited parenthetically.

26. Susan Willis, *A Primer for Daily Life* (New York: Routledge, 1991), p. 100.

27. Nancy Armstrong, *Desire and Domestic Fiction* (Oxford: Oxford University Press, 1989) p. 95.

28. This is the gist of Laura Brown's argument, especially in chapter 6 of *Ends of Empire:Women and Ideology in Early Eighteenth-Century English Literature* (Ithaca: Cornell University Press, 1993).

29. Alexander Pope, *The Rape of the Lock and Other Poems*. ed. Geoffrey Tillotson (New Haven: Yale University Press, 1962), canto 1, lines 129–36.

30. Edward Said sets the stage for a reexamination of eighteenth-century literature and culture when he writes, "How do writers in the period before the 'scramble for Africa,' say, situate and see themselves and their work in the larger world? We shall find them using striking but careful strategies, many of them derived from expected sources—positive ideas of home, of a nation and its language, of proper order, good behavior, moral virtues." See *Culture and Imperialism* (New York: Knopf, 1993), p. 81.

31. See, for example, Abena Busia, "Silencing Sycorax," *Cultural Critique* (1989–1990), pp. 81–104.

32. Indeed, Deidre Lynch argues that this scene represents Camilla as "the accidental consumer." She explains that this episode is significant because Camilla is engaged in conduct that is

historically "in the vanguard of consumer practice and conduct that, in slightly altered circumstances, would express what recent cultural criticism identifies as a new consumer subjectivity." See her essay entitled "Frances Burney and Feminist Agoraphobia," delivered at the Modern Language Association in December 1994, San Diego.

33. For a full discussion of "the ineffable psychological subtexts of selfhood" in this novel, see Lynch's work.

34. I am citing John Fiske, *Power Plays, Power Works* (London: Verso, 1993), p. 70. De Certeau discusses "la perruque" in *The Practice of Everyday Life*, trans. Steven de Rendall (Berkeley: University of California Press, 1984), pp. 24–28.

Pornography

1. Lynn Hunt, "Introduction," *The Invention of Pornography: Obscenity and the Origins of Modernity* (New York: Zone, 1993), p. 42. Douglas Stewart observes a crucial shift in the "metaphor system" of pornography in the late eighteenth-century. For him, pornography was "not even ideologically possible before the rise of capitalism, and it flourishes only because capitalism flourishes, for it is the logical extension of capitalistic ideals of rationalized production, efficiency, and maximized profit." "Pornography, Obscenity, and Capitalism," *Antioch Review* (1977), 35:399–400. For both Stewart and Robert Markley, Cleland's *Fanny Hill* provides a rich opportunity for the study of the late eighteenth-century ideological construction of sexuality. See Markley's essay, "Language, Power, and Sexuality in Cleland's *Fanny Hill*," *Philological Quarterly* (1984), 63:343–56.

2. Peter Wagner, *Eros Revived: Erotica of the Enlightenment in England and America* (London: Secker and Warburg, 1988), p. 6.

3. Walter Kendrick, *The Secret Museum: Pornography in Modern Culture* (New York: Penguin, 1987), p. 2. According to Kendrick, it was the discovery and subsequent naming of the "priceless obscenities" of Pompeii that gave rise to the first modern coinage of the word in English in 1850 (p. 11).

4. Obviously, the bibliography on this controversial subject is enormous. However, the antipornography position is still best articulated in the work of Catherine MacKinnon, for example, in her essay "Not as Moral Issue," *Yale Law and Policy Review* (1984), 11:321–45. On the other side, see Kate Ellis, with Nan Hunter, Beth Baker, Barbara O'Dair, and Abby Tallmer, *Caught Looking: Feminism, Pornography, and Censorship* (New York: Feminist Anti-Censorship Taskforce [FACT] Book Committee, 1986); Alison Assiter and Avendon Carol, eds., *Bad Girls and Dirty Pictures: The Challenge to Reclaim Feminism* (London: Pluto, 1993).

5. See Leo Bersani, *A Future for Astyanax: Character and Desire in Literature* (Boston: Little, Brown, 1976), p. 296. According to John de St. Jorre, *L'Histoire d'O* was, in fact, written by a woman, Dominique Aury, who produced the book for her lover, Jean Paulhan, because she feared losing him. He called it "the most ardent love letter any man has ever received." *New Yorker*, August 1, 1994, pp. 42–50.

6. Linda Williams, *Hard Core: Power, Pleasure, and the Frenzy of the Visible* (Berkeley: University of California Press, 1989), pp. 113–14.

7. I argue this in contrast to Nancy Miller on p. 53 of her essay entitled "The I's in Drag: The Sex of Recollection," *The Eighteenth Century: Theory and Interpretation* (1981), 22:47–57.

8. For a different use of the semiotic square in reference to the female body, see Susan Green, "Semiotic Modalities of the Female Body in Aphra Behn's *The Dutch Lover*," in Heidi Hutner, ed., *Rereading Aphra Behn* (Charlottesville: University of Virginia Press, 1993), pp. 121–47.

9. Laura Brown provides a comprehensive overview of this shift. See *Ends of Empire:Women and Ideology in Early Eighteenth-Century English Literature* (Ithaca: Cornell University Press, 1993), pp. 89–97.

10. The most obvious example of such misogynist discourse is Joseph Swetnam's *The Arraignment of Lewde, Idle, Forward, and Unconstant Women . . .* (London: Edward Allde for Thomas Archer, 1615). For a discussion of early feminist responses to such misogynist diatribe, see Hilda Smith, *Reason's Disciples: Seventeenth-Century English Feminists* (Urbana: University of Illinois Press, 1982), chapter 2.

11. For an interesting survey of the relationship between "communications technology" and pornography, see John Tierney, "Porn, the Low-Slung Engine of Progress," *NewYork Times*, Sunday, January 9, 1994, section 2, p. 1.

12. See *The Amorous Illustrations of Thomas Rowlandson*, with an introduction by Gert Schiff (New York: Cythera, 1969), hereafter cited as *AI*; and *The Forbidden Erotic of Thomas Rowlandson*, with an introduction by Kurt von Meier (Los Angeles: Hogarth Guild, 1970), hereafter cited as *TFE*.

13. This print could also be compared to "Love Play" (*TFE* 93), where the female figure swings toward a grotesque male, with his breeches down around his knees. Though the plates are slightly different, the expression on the woman's face is the same in both.

14. Reproduced here from the *Caricature Magazine*, this print is also called "British Goods at Auction in Calcutta," and it exists in another version done by James Gillray in 1786. See Dorothy George, *Catalogue of Political and Personal Satires* (London: British Museum Publications, 1978), p. 336. Still, von Meier asserts that Rowlandson's version may be dated as early as 1785. The Gillray version has a few minor differences: the expressions on both the central woman's and black boy's faces differ, for example. Its message is, nonetheless, nearly identical to Rowlandson's, and both versions perform the same cultural work.

15. George, *Catalogue*, p. 336.

Businesswomen

1. Samuel Richardson, *Clarissa, or the History of a Young Lady*, ed. Angus Ross (NewYork: Penguin, 1985 [1747–1748]), p. 1388.

2. On the connection between words and the copiousness of the female body, see Patricia Parker, *Literary Fat Ladies: Rhetoric, Gender, and Property* (New York: Methuen, 1987).

3. For a fuller analysis of Mrs. Sinclair's role as bawd, see Robert A. Erickson, *Mother Midnight: Birth, Sex, and Fate in Eighteenth-Century Fiction* (NewYork: AMS, 1986); or Judith Wilt, "He Could No Farther: A Modest Proposal About Lovelace and Clarissa," *PMLA* (1977), 92:19–32.

4. The process I trace here parallels the change described by Deborah Valenze in *The First Industrial Woman* (New York: Oxford University Press, 1995). As Valenze writes, " After mid-century, the positive image of the laboring woman characterized by her industriousness and economic potential was challenged by another, more critical view: she came to embody the undesirable

impulses of human nature, including a general disregard for morality and the law, particularly as it related to property" (p. 26). Whereas Valenze documents the actual historical circumstances that brought about the marginalization of the working woman, I am interested in tracing discursive shifts.

5. On gendering the mortal human body as female, see Dorothy Dinnerstein, *The Mermaid and the Minotaur: Sexual Arrangement and Human Malaise* (New York: Harper and Row, 1976).

6. Olwen Hufton, "Survey Articles, Women in History. 1. Early Modern Europe," *Past and Present* (1983), 101:132.

7. Bridget Hill, *Women, Work, and Sexual Politics in Eighteenth-Century England* (Oxford: Basil Blackwell, 1989), p. 86.

8. *A Complete Guide to All Persons Who Have Any* TRADE *or* CONCERN *with the City of London and Parts of Adjacent London* (London: Hitch, Hawes et alia, 1760).

9. Peter Earle, *The Making of the English Middle Class* (Los Angeles: The University of California Press, 1989), p. 159. Earle explains, "The wife's separate estate was normally created by either a contract entered into by prospective husband and wife before marriage or by conveying property to friends of the wife, who would hold it in trust for her use." Working from a source entitled *Aris's Gazette, Advertisements of Trade Announcements, 1750–1796,* Maxine Berg compiled a list of "widows announcing intention of carrying on business of deceased husbands." Among the trades the widows planned to pursue were plumber and glazier, iron monger, and japanned clock dial manufacturer. See "Women's Work, Mechanization and the Early Phases of Industrialization in England," in Patrick Joyce, ed., *The Historical Meanings of Work* (Cambridge: Cambridge University Press, 1987), p. 97. In the eighteenth-century Daniel Defoe had been an advocate for women learning their husbands' trades. Warning them of the possibility of becoming "tradesman's widows," he feared that the wives would be "beholden" to apprentices upon their husbands' death and, as result, have sexual relations with them. See *The Complete English Tradesman in Familiar Letters*, 2 vols. (London: Charles Rivington, 1726–1727), 1:353.

10. Alice Clark, *Working Life of Women in the Seventeenth Century* (New York: Harcourt, Brace and Howe, 1920), pp. 6–7.

11. Hill, *Women, Work, and Sexual Politics*, pp. 260 and 263. The work of Ivy Pinchbeck also follows the same basic narrative. See *Women Workers and the Industrial Revolution* (New York: Augustus M. Kelley, 1969).

12. Valenze, *The First Industrial Woman*, chapters 3 and 4. I cite p. 69.

13. Berg, "Women's Work," p. 89.

14. Keith Snell, *Annals of the Laboring Poor* (Cambridge: Cambridge University Press, 1985), p. 272.

15. Peter Earle, "The Female Labour Market in London in the Late Seventeenth and Early Eighteenth Centuries," *Economic History Review* (1989), 42:331.

16. See Louis Althusser, "Ideology and Ideological State Apparatuses," *Lenin and Philosophy,* trans. Ben Brewer (New York: Monthly Review Press, 1971), pp. 127–86.

17. *A General Description of the Trades Digested in Alphabetical Order* (London: T. Waller, 1747); "The Tradesman's Dictionary" in *The General Shop Book; or, The Tradesman's Universal Director. Being a Most Useful and Necessary Compendium to Lie Upon the Counter of Every* SHOPKEEPER, *Whether Wholesale or*

Retail, in Town or Country (London: Hitch and Hawes, 1753); R. Campbell, *The London Tradesman* (London: T. Gardner, 1747). Further references are cited parenthetically.

18. Snell, *Annals of the Laboring Poor*, pp. 279–82.

19. *The General Shop Book* specifies, in contrast, "This work is done chiefly by women." Campbell, *The London Tradesman*, p. 153, writes, "[Embroidery] is chiefly performed by Women; it is an ingenious Art, requires a nice Taste in Drawing, a bold Fancy to invent new patterns, and a clean Hand to save their Work from tarnishing it." The difference may have arisen over the type of embroidery, whether it occurred on a waistcoat or bodice, and so on.

20. Campbell, *The London Tradesman*, p. 224.

21. *The General Shop Book.*

22. The historical Semiramis was an Assyrian queen, credited with irrigating Babylon and various military endeavors. The legendary Semiramis was thought to have been ruler of an empire. She figures frequently in misogynist discourse as an emasculator of men. In *Eunuchism Display'd*, for example, Charles Ancillon blames Semiramis for being the first to create the castrato (London: E. Curll, 1718).

23. Though it would seem to have been current later, the OED cites the last usage of *business* as a euphemism for sexual intercourse in 1654. See *The Compact Edition of the Oxford English Dictionary*, 2 vols. (New York: Oxford University Press, 1971), 1:1206.

24. John Cleland, *Memoirs of a Woman of Pleasure*, ed. Peter Sabor (New York: Oxford University Press, 1985 [1748]), p. 83.

25. Fanny Burney, *The Wanderer*, ed. Margaret Anne Doody and Peter Sabor (New York: Oxford University Press, 1991 [1814]), pp. 427–28.

26. Valenze, *The First Industrial Woman*, p. 139. I draw here from her chapter 7.

27. George Lillo, *The London Merchant, or The History of George Barnwell*, in *The Dramatic Works of George Lillo*, ed. James L. Steffensen (Oxford: Oxford University Press, 1993). Further references are cited parenthetically by act and scene.

28. Or, as Alexander Catcott writes in "The Antiquity and Honourableness of the Practice of Merchandize: A SERMON Preached Before the Worshipful Society of Merchants of Bristol" (Bristol, 1744), "Besides, an intercourse with other nations, or even an account brought us of their learning, trade, government, and the like, enlarges and enriches the mind, and cures men of that self-conceit and roughness both of temper and behavior, that is the result of ignorance of men and manners."

29. Defoe, *The Complete English Tradesman in Familiar Letters*, 1:153

30. Malachy Postlethwayt and James Royson, *The British Mercantile Academy or The Accomplished Merchant* (London: John and Paul Knapton, 1750). Further references are cited parenthetically. For alternative accounts of how the business community constructed itself, see James Raven, *Judging New Wealth: Popular Publishing and Responses to Commerce in England, 1750–1800* (Oxford: Clarendon Press, 1992); John McVeagh, *Tradefull Merchants: The Portrayal of the Capitalism in Literature* (Boston: Routledge and Kegan Paul, 1981); and Neil McKendrick, " 'Gentleman and Players' Revisited: The Gentlemanly Ideal, the Business Ideal, and the Professional Ideal in England," in Neil McKendrick and R. B. Outhwaite, ed., *Business Life and Public Policy* (Cambridge: Cambridge University Press, 1986), pp. 98–136. Generally apologetic for the idea of the businessman,

none of these scholars takes into consideration the role of gender in the discursive construction of business.

31. Cf. Leonore Davidoff and Catherine Hall: "The valuation of actions and materials in monetary terms were regarded as a quintessentially masculine skill and prerogative. Such expertise was an essential part of the middle-class challenge to the aristocratic male whose skills lay with gambling, duelling, sporting, and sexual prowess. The accomplishments of middle-class men were primarily sedentary and literate, the manipulation of the pen and the ruler rather than the sword and gun. They implied a cerebral control of the world but were no less effective in yielding economic rewards which could lead to wealth and power." *Family Fortunes: Men and Women of the English Middle Class, 1780–1850* (Chicago: University of Chicago Press, 1987), p. 205.

32. The gradual historical movement toward the image of the disembodied corporation fits into this idea.

33. See Ernest Becker, *The Denial of Death* (New York: Basic, 1973); Dinnerstein, *The Mermaid and the Minotaur*; Mary Russo, *The Female Grotesque: Risk, Excess, and Modernity* (New York: Routledge, 1995); Gail Kern Paster, *The Body Embarrassed: Drama and the Disciplines of Shame in Early Modern England* (Ithaca: Cornell University Press, 1993).

Prostitutes

1. See Robert A. Erickson, *Mother Midnight: Birth, Sex, and Fate in Eighteenth-Century Fiction* (New York: AMS, 1986), pp. 140–47, for a discussion of Richardson's sources.

2. Ibid., p. 145.

3. *Nocturnal Revels, or the History of King's-Palace, and Other Modern Nunneries, Containing their Mysteries, Devotions, and Sacrifices* by a Monk of the Order of Saint Francis (London: M. Goadby, 1779); see also Fernando Henriques, *Prostitution in Europe and the New World* (London: MacGibbon and Kee, 1963), chapter 5.

4. M. D'Archenholz, *A Picture of England: Containing a Description of the Laws, Customs, and Manners of England* (Dublin: P. Byre, 1790), p. 189. The fact that Mrs. Sinclair is so easily able to have Clarissa arrested for her debts bears out this traveler's assertion concerning the relation of prostitutes to the law.

5. Roy Porter, *English Society in the Eighteenth Century* (New York: Penguin, 1982), p. 382.

6. Sean Shesgreen identifies Creswell as "one the most famous procuresses in London between the Restoration and the Revolution." She is the same Madam Creswell who provides instruction to the novice in *The Whore's Rhetoric* (1683). See *The Criers and Hawkers of London* (Stanford: Stanford University Press, 1990), p. 178.

7. See, for example, a poem written in response to Hogarth, entitled *The Harlot's Progress or the Humors of Drury Lane in Six Cantos*, 3d ed. (London: B. Dickinson, 1732). Even a poem like "The Magdalens: An Elegy," written to sympathize with the plight of penitent prostitutes, draws on Hogarth (London: R. and J. Dodsley, 1763).

8. *The Compact Edition of the Oxford English Dictionary* (New York: Oxford University Press, 1971), 1:178.

9. The parallel in the popular imagination today is, of course, the black pimp, whose body is similarly used to fixate attention on the evils of prostitution. Erickson opens up a fascinating dis-

cussion about the connections between the bawd and the midwife, who were historically linked in more ways than one.

10. On the grotesque, see Peter Stallybrass and Allon White, *The Politics and Poetics of Transgression* (Ithaca: Cornell University Press, 1986); and Mary Russo, "Female Grotesques: Carnival and Theory," in Teresa de Lauretis, ed., *Feminist Studies / Critical Studies* (Bloomington: Indiana University Press, 1986), pp. 213–29.

11. See Laura Brown, *Ends of Empire:Women and Ideology in Early Eighteenth-Century English Literature* (Ithaca: Cornell, 1993), chapter 6.

12. Dryden's translation of Vergil's *Aeneid*, as cited in Samuel Richardson, *Clarissa, or the History of a Young Lady*, ed. Angus Ross (New York: Penguin, 1985).

13. Catherine Gallagher, "George Eliot and Daniel Deronda: The Prostitute and the Jewish Question," in Ruth Yeazell, ed., *Sex, Politics, and Science in the Nineteenth-Century Novel* (Baltimore: Johns Hopkins University Press, 1986), p. 41

14. Mary Douglas, *Purity and Danger: An Analysis of Concepts of Pollution and Taboo* (New York: Praeger, 1966), pp. 2, 4.

15. From Daniel Defoe's *Roxana*, for instance, one learns virtually nothing about the physical conditions of the prostitute's life. And while *The Harlot's Progress* illustrates very well the physical decline that resulted from venereal disease, it says nothing about the particulars of sex work: where and how does Moll Hackabout find her customers? How much do they pay her? And so on. My thinking on this issue is indebted to Shannon Bell's *Reading,Writing, and Rewriting the Prostitute's Body* (Bloomington: Indiana University Press, 1994).

16. Three good examples of reformist texts are: Robert Dingley, *Mr. Dingley's Proposals for Establishing a Public Place of Reception for Penitent Prostitutes* (London: W. Fader, 1758); Jonas Hanway, *Letter V to Robert Dingley. esq., Being a Proposal for the Relief and Employment of Friendless Girls and Prostitutes* (London: R. and J. Dodsley, 1758); and Saunders Welch, *A Proposal to Render Effectual a Plan to Remove the Nuisance of Common Prostitutes from the Streets of this Metropolis* (London: C. Henderson, 1758). Further references to Welch's essay will be cited parenthetically. In "Dr. Johnson and Saunders Welch's *Proposals*," E. L. McAdam discusses the authorship of Welch's essay. *R. E.S.* (1953), 4:337–45.

17. Welch, *A Proposal to Render Effectual,* p. 19.

18. D'Archenholz, *A Picture of England,* p. 193.

19. The notion of containment is visualized very well in an illustration of Magdelan Chapel, done by Thomas Rowlandson in *The Microcosm of London in Miniature,* 3 vols. (T. Bensley, 1808–1810). In the illustration, reformed prostitutes are depicted at the center of a highly organized geometric architecture. With patrons on all sides, they sit at rigid attention during the Sunday service.

20. Mary Wollstonecraft, *A Vindication of the Rights of Woman*, ed. Carol Poston (New York: Norton, 1975 [1792]), p. 71.

21. John Fielding, *A Plan for a Preservatory and Reformatory For the Benefit of Deserted Girls and Penitent Prostitutes* (R. Franklin, 1758), pp. 19–20.

22. Jonas Hanway, *Letter V to Robert Dingley Being a Proposal for the Relief and Employment of Friendless Girls and Repenting Prostitutes* (London: R and J Dodsley, 1758), p. 15.

23. For further discussion of the rehabilitation of prostitutes, see Donna T. Andrew, *Philanthropy and the Police: London Charity in the Eighteenth Century* (Princeton: Princeton University Press, 1989), pp. 119–127.

24. Bernard Mandeville, *A Modest Defense of Public Stewes: Or An Essay on Whoring* (London: A. Moore, 1734), p. 9. Further references are cited parenthetically.

25. In nineteenth-century France, as Charles Bernheimer writes, reformers like Alexandre Parent-Duchatelet continued to look for physiological evidence of the prostitute's profession: Parent felt "it would be ideal if an examination of a woman's sexual organs could ascertain, by the degree of distention of the vagina or the enlargement of the clitoris, that the organs had been subjected to an abnormally high incidence of use." See *Figures of Ill-Repute: Representing Prostitution in Nineteenth-Century France* (Cambridge: Harvard University Press, 1989), p. 24.

26. She elaborates, "The whores appearing on Mandeville's pages are filthy embodiments of and containers for the kind of pleasure that one must deny one gets from profit-intensive business management: indolence and pleasure in excess are here figured as sexual pleasure, and sexual pleasure is quarantined, as it were, from the clean concerns of business." Parallel to the argument I am making here, Laura Mandell provides a Marxist account of how the discourse of capitalism employs gender: in "Bawds and Merchants: Engendering Capitalist Desires" *ELH* (1992), 59:117, 116.

27. For a discussion of the similar interruption of the feminine into a masculine discursive process, see Bernheimer, *Figures of Ill-Repute,* chapter 1.

28. See, for example, the work of Susan Bordo, especially *Unbearable Weight: Feminism, Western Culture, and the Body* (Berkeley: University of California Press, 1993).

29. For a feminist critique of the multinational corporation, see, for example, Cynthia Enloe's *Bananas, Beaches, and Feminists: Making Feminist Sense of International Politics* (Berkeley: University of California Press, 1989).

Conclusion

1. "Paris is Burning," produced and directed by Jennie Livingston (Chatsworth, Cal.: Academy/Image Entertainment, 1992).

2. Among other studies, Mary Poovey's *Uneven Developments: The Ideological Work of Gender in Mid-Victorian England* documents this shift (Chicago: University of Chicago Press, 1988).

3. Venus appears to be Hispanic.

4. In a compelling example the medical profession recently decreed that insurance tables, which had been revised upward in the 1980s to allow for heavier body weights in Americans, were unduly generous: in fact, Americans as a whole needed to weigh *less*. The media discussion that ensued, much of it concerning the need to curb inordinate appetites, seems richly metaphorical in an economic climate where "undisciplined" Americans are thought to spend too much and save too little.

5. The phrase comes from Rémy Saisselin's description of Marshall Field's creation: "the new woman, member of the social set, later of the Junior Council, and part of the new elite that in the United States would set the fashions and moral values for other women." See *The Bourgeois and the Bibelot* (New Brunswick: Rutgers University Press, 1984), p. 36.

6. Ibid., pp. 35 and 42.

7. Rachel Bowlby, *Just Looking: Consumer Culture in Dreiser, Gissing, and Zola* (New York: Methuen, 1985), pp. 11 and 28.

8. Saisselin, *The Bourgeois and the Bibelot*, p. 53.

9. Anne Friedberg, *Window Shopping: Cinema and the Postmodern* (Berkeley: University of California Press, 1993), p. 2.

10. Ibid., pp. 32–37.

11. Ibid., p. 118.

12. Or, as Judith Williamson writes, "Consuming seems to offer a certain scope for creativity, rather like a toy where all the parts are pre-chosen but the combinations are multiple," in *Consuming Passions: The Dynamics of Popular Culture* (London: Marion Boyars, 1986), p. 230.

13. Mica Nava, "Consumerism and Its Contradictions," *Cultural Studies* (1987), 1:205.

14. Betty Friedan, *The Feminine Mystique* (New York: Dell, 1963), p. 330.

15. Susan Douglas, *Where the Girls Are: Growing Up Female with the Mass Media* (New York: Times, 1994), p. 14. In an endnote to this passage Douglas cites the work of Barbara Ehreneich, Elizabeth Hess, and Gloria Jacobs.

16. Ibid., p. 246.

17. Since the time this was written, the Pleasant Company has developed an additional product line: the American Girl of Today. The customer can choose from a total of twenty different possible dolls heads, with a range of racial and ethnic features. These dolls are accompanied by six blank books in which a personalized story can be written.

18. Susan S. Adler, *Meet Samantha: An American Girl* (Middleton, Wis.: Pleasant, 1986), pp. 58–59.

19. *The American Girls Collection, Spring Collection 1995* (Middleton, Wis.: Pleasant, 1995), p. 4.

20. Ibid., p. 4.

21. Connie Porter, *Meet Addy: An American Girl* (Middleton, Wis.: Pleasant, 1995), p. 21.

22. *The American Girls Collection*, pp. 28 and 27.

23. See the witty satirical piece by Susan Shapiro entitled "My Mentor, Barbie," *New York Times Magazine*, November 6, 1994, p. 84. Among other claims, Shapiro asserts that Barbie taught her "A shortage of men won't ruin the party" and "It's cool to have many careers."

Index